BOUNCE BACK TOO

God is our refuge and strength, an ever-present help in trouble. (Psalm 46:1)

TRAGEDY? DISAPPOINTMENT? FAILURE?
YOU CAN . . .

BOUNCE
BACK
TOO

— COMPILED BY —
DIANA L. JAMES

HORIZON BOOKS
CAMP HILL, PENNSYLVANIA

Horizon Books
3825 Hartzdale Drive, Camp Hill, PA 17011
www.cpi-horizon.com

ISBN: 0-88965-155-8

Printed in the United States of America

98 99 00 01 02   5 4 3 2 1

To my husband, Max James,
with appreciation for his loving
encouragement and for his creative
and meticulous editorial assistance.

Contents

Acknowledgments...xi

Introduction...1

Chapter 1   Faith: The Essential Ingredient

The Faith of a Child   *Florence Littauer* 5

Yes, I Can!   *Diana L. James* 13

Chapter 2   Attitude: The Life Conditioner

Seeds of Peace   *Max Lucado*..21

The Nurse and the Mountain   *Shirley Doan* 27

Breakthrough to Joy   *C. Christopher Knippers* 33

Overload   *Emilie Barnes* 41

Are You Ready for a Great Day?   *Cassandra Woods* 45

Finding the Power to Keep Loving   *Gary Smalley*.............49

The Blessed Blizzard   *Joyce A. Minatra* 55

Chapter 3   Facing Fear and Failure

The Ability to Fail   *Tim Hansel* 61

The Perfect Size   *Paula Mitchell* 67

He's Always There   *Kathie Clarke* 73

To Overcome Fear—Just Do It!   *Douglas A. Clark*...........77

Chapter 4   Healing Family Relationships

The Language of Love   *Laura Sabin Riley* 85

The Lost Years   *Marie Asner* 89

The Woman Who Wouldn't Be Loved   *Caron Loveless* 93

In Search of a Father   *Chris Bennett* 99

Never Give Up   *Carol Neidhardt* 105

Second-Chance Parenting   *Karen O'Connor* 109

Chapter 5   Growing through Grief

Times of Joy and Sorrow   *Fred Littauer* 117

The Vacuum   *Suzy Ryan* 125

For They Shall Be Comforted   *Gwen Bagne* 131

Chapter 6   Overcoming Financial Stress

True Financial Freedom   *Paul J. Lauterjung* 139

Money—No Small Change   *Andy and Vivian Baniak* 145

In God I Trust   *Gisele Guilbert* 151

From Worry to Trust   *Betty J. Price* 157

Chapter 7   Meeting Physical Challenge

I Will Still Praise You   *Jo Franz* 163

There Is Hope   *Terry and Jo Cotter* 171

The Gift   *Linda Shepherd* 177

But I Know Who Takes Care
     of Lives   *Vincent Kituku* 183

One Day at a Time!   *Dianne McGarey* 189

Do You Want to Be Well?   *Bruce Larson* 195

Chapter 8   The Healing Balm of Forgiveness

The Servant As a Forgiver   *Charles R. Swindoll* 203

"You'd Better Be Good!"   *Marlene Bagnull* 209

Grace on a Saturday Afternoon   *Beverly Bush Smith* 213

Bricks in Your Backpack   *Zig Ziglar* 219

Chapter 9   The Joy of Helping Others

Kinder Than Kind   *Jerry B. Jenkins* 227

These Are My Children   *Beverly Hamel* 231

The Turning Point   *Leila McDougal* 235

Unexpected Curves   *Patty Stump* 241

Why Am I Lonely?   *Greg Laurie* 247

Acknowledgments

Thank you to all the kind and generous people who contributed stories for this book.

Thank you to the many friends who prayed for me and for the book as it was being compiled.

Thank you to my brother, David, my four sons, David, Rick, Robert and Glen and my "buddies": Bonnie, JJ, Norma and Jana (and of course, Max)—all of whom have been my cheering section and my boosters throughout this and my other writing projects.

Bless you, bless you, one and all.

Introduction

The book you now hold in your hands is an instrument of hope. If you have experienced discouragement, fear, failure, physical challenge, financial problems or grief, you will be encouraged as you read—these people have been there, too.

Many of the writers included here have had their beliefs or their attitudes tested. Some have lost their faith and even voiced their anger at God. All have come through these experiences with a more profound understanding and appreciation of God's love and His forgiving grace.

This book is a sequel to my first book, *Whatever Happens, You Too Can BOUNCE BACK*. Readers of that book, Christians and non-Christians alike, people coming from a variety of backgrounds and many walks of life, related to *BOUNCE BACK's* stories of hope and encouragement and asked for more. This time, I have included a larger number of stories written by men, many of whom are well-known and highly respected pastors, authors and speakers. I am highly honored to present their stories, but honored as well to have stories from all the contributors, whether unknown, little known or renowned. Each contribution is a blessing in its own way.

Faith, whether expressed or implied, is the underlying theme of every story in this book. It is the essential ingredient in "bouncing back" from the trials, setbacks, despair and deep concerns that sometimes beset us. But what is faith, and how do we find it?

As Florence Littauer describes it in the first chapter, we see faith in the bright-eyed, unshakable trust of a little child. We see it also in the faith of mature adults who have appropriated that same childlike faith in the face of an impending disaster. What we learn (or are reminded of) from reading "The Faith of a Child" is that faith goes a step beyond simply believing: *It is acting on or resting upon that belief.*

The second story is my own account of how, by *asking* for it in prayer, I found the faith to persevere in the face of paralyzing self-doubt. In so doing, I rediscovered God's power to provide inner strength and lift me from despair.

Throughout the other chapters, you will find accounts of life-changing events and insights gained by people who went through difficulties, perhaps wandering in the wilderness for a while, but who ultimately bounced back to joyful, fruitful lives.

My prayer is that you who read this book—whether looking for inspiration, searching for answers or seeking a comforting word of hope—will find herein a blessing, a benediction and a message that will minister to your need.

— DLJ

The LORD will give strength unto his people;
the LORD will bless his people with peace.
(Psalm 29:11, KJV)

Chapter 1

Faith:
The Essential Ingredient

Faith is the substance of things hoped for, the evidence of things not seen. (Hebrews 11:1, KJV)

The Faith of a Child

Florence Littauer

riday the 13th began for us at 6:17 a.m. with an earthquake. As we were jolted awake, my husband Fred turned on the radio and heard that besides the earthquake, a forest fire had started in Big Bear, a mountain community twenty miles away. As the day progressed, so did the fires, fanned by forty-mph winds. By 5 p.m., when I put the meat in the oven for a company dinner, I looked out to see the entire sky behind Mt. McKinley a bright orange. The radio reports ominously told how hot, hurricane-force winds were wildly blasting the fire out of control, heading it toward homes in the northeast section of San Bernardino—where we lived.

At 6:30 p.m. our little six-year-old Freddie, who had been listening closely to the radio, called us and our dinner guests into the living room and announced we were going to have a prayer meeting. He moved our antique prayer bench into the cen-

ter of the room and stood behind it like a little pastor in a pulpit. He opened in prayer, then handed
me the family Bible and said, "Mother, read us
something from the Bible that tells us we'll be safe
from the fire." It was quite an assignment, and I
struggled to find a verse that would show God
would save our home. Then I remembered Psalm
91:5-7: "Thou shalt not be afraid for the terror by
night; nor for the arrow that flieth by day; nor for
the pestilence that walketh in darkness; nor for the
destruction that wasteth at noonday. A thousand
shall fall at thy side, and ten thousand at thy right
hand; but it shall not come nigh thee" (KJV).

We prayed and claimed the promise that the fire
would not come nigh unto us. We also claimed verse
10: "There shall no evil befall thee, neither shall any
plague come nigh thy dwelling" (KJV).

We then saw God's condition. He states that if
we put Him first in times of plenty, He will care
for us in times of danger: "Because he hath set his
love upon me, therefore will I deliver him: I will
set him on high, because he hath known my name.
He shall call upon me, and I will answer him"
(91:14-15, KJV).

As Freddie stood behind the bench, he pointed
to each one of us in order and asked us to pray for
our home. He concluded our meeting by thanking
God ahead of time for the miracle He was going
to perform. I knew then the Lord would save us—
if only to reward the faith of this little child.

When our last guests arrived at 7 p.m., we chatted over the clatter of fire trucks racing up our street. Before long we were startled by heavy footsteps on our front deck. Two big firemen knocked on the front door. "Prepare to evacuate," they said as I opened the door. "The fire has whipped up the back of Mt. McKinley, and as soon as it comes over the top, you'll have to leave."

At exactly 8 o'clock, the first flames fanned over the summit and we left the dinner table to watch as the whole crest of the mountain was quickly outlined in fire. It was a majestic sight. The flames advanced in a straight path from as far as we could see, left and right, heading down the mountainside to the canyon below us. As I stood on the redwood deck watching the approaching fire, a fireman said, "Only a miracle could save this house."

The police made a roadblock at the bottom of the hill and only residents and relatives were allowed through. In order to get up the hill, our friends told the police they were our brothers and sisters. (Later the officers said, "I never knew anyone to have so many brothers and sisters!") Several friends came with trucks ready to move us out and some came to take our children home with them.

Freddie refused to leave. He wanted to stay and see the miracle he knew was about to happen. Our daughter Lauren, unaware of our danger, was cheering at a high school football game many miles away, and her younger sister Marita was already at a friend's home for the night.

At 9 p.m. Marita ran into the house and gath-

ered up her two cages of pet mice to take back to
her girlfriend's house.

"Don't you have any faith?" I called.

"I do," she said, "but the mice don't, so I'm taking them with me."

By this time the whole street was a mass of confusion. Policemen evacuated hysterical women
and excited children; people with hastily rented
moving vans loaded up priceless furnishings; one
woman threw her sterling silver into the swimming pool. A reporter for the local newspaper,
Harvey Feit, worked his way up the street
through the turmoil to our house. When he inter-
viewed us, he was amazed at the calm and joyful
attitude in our home.

"How do you feel about your house being destroyed?" Harvey asked.

He was stunned at Fred's confident answer.
"The Lord won't let my house burn. He gave it to
us, and we use it for His work. If He wants it to
stand, it will stand."

"Do you share your husband's faith that this
house is not going to burn?" asked Harvey.

"Yes," I said with an assurance I'd never known
before. I could hardly wait to see how the Lord
was going to do it.

During the long evening Fred made more coffee. There was an air of expectancy as we—family, friends and firemen—sipped, watched and
prayed.

Throughout our home and on the roof, groups
of friends gathered in prayer, and a few strangers

who wandered in to watch remained to pray, several for the first time in their lives. A teenage boy, Paul Britton from across the street, asked Christ to come into his heart while standing on our roof holding a fire hose. Because of his commitment that night, both his mother and father later became believing Christians and are now involved in Christian work.

About 10:30 the firemen insisted that all children leave before the fire reached our home. As Freddie kissed me good-bye, he whispered, "I'm sorry I can't stay to take care of you, Mother, but I'll be back as soon as it's over."

At 11 p.m. Lauren ran through the crowd, flung her arms around me and sobbed for joy to see me alive. She had been coming back to San Bernardino on the bus from the football game and suddenly realized the fire was burning "our mountain." By this time the fire had reached the bottom of the canyon nearest us and was starting up.

As the sixty-mph winds moved the fire in a massive march toward our house, firemen turned on the hoses for the first time. I looked out the kitchen window and saw an olive tree not twenty feet away burst into flames. A fireman told me I had to get out, as the house would probably explode any minute. I kissed Fred good-bye and, with my Bible in hand, walked through the kitchen where a friend was pouring a cup of coffee. I'll never forget his question: "I hate to bother you at a time like this, but where do you keep your sugar?" I thought it hardly mattered whether his coffee had sugar or not, but I stopped long enough to hand him the sugar bowl.

As Lauren and I ran through the smoke to our car, the reporter called, "How does your faith look now?" We glanced back and saw the cliff behind the house flare up in a fence of fire and then, as the smoke enshrouded the silhouette, we could see the house no more. As we drove out of the yard, the firemen lifted the hoses over the car, making an archway to escape. We left knowing Fred and his best friend Ralph Wagoner were still inside.

Twenty minutes later, after a slow trip through the traffic to a friend's home, I called Fred and was relieved when he picked up the phone.

"Praise the Lord," he said, "the house is still here!" He then explained in jubilation how, as the hurricane-force winds whipped up the hill, the direction had suddenly changed, splitting the fire in two, sending half of it up the cliff behind the house and the rest down to the ravine below. For twenty minutes the smoke and flames had enveloped our home as Fred and his faithful friend Ralph watched through the windows and prayed for the Lord to save the house. Harvey Feit told Fred later that as he saw the flames shooting over the roof of the house, he was afraid it was gone. But then the smoke cleared, and he said he looked in disbelief as the house came into view—whole and unharmed. God had covered our home with His protective hand.

Editor's note: Freddie is the Littauers' adopted son, adopted after the loss of their first two sons. See Fred Littauer's story in Chapter 4.

Excerpted and abridged from I've Found My Keys, Now Where's My Car? *Florence Littauer, Copyright 1994, Thomas Nelson Publishers, Nashville, TN.*

And a little child shall lead them. (Isaiah 11:6, KJV)

Florence Littauer, founder of CLASS (Christian Leaders, Authors and Speakers Seminars, Inc.), is a best-selling author of over twenty-five books. With her husband Fred, she travels nationally and internationally as a Christian speaker, sharing her humor and valuable insights. Florence is also in demand as a radio and TV talk show guest and keynote speaker for retreats, business conventions and seminars. Between their travels, Florence and Fred reside in Palm Springs, California.

Yes, I Can!

Diana L. James

*D*awn crept softly over a misty, gray horizon as I paced beside the window of my lonely hotel room. Darkness turned to light, revealing my pile of neatly organized speech notes on the table.

I had been awake for hours, my mind racing: *Why am I here? I don't want to do this. I'm not ready. I'm not good enough. I'm going to make a fool of myself! Why did I get myself into this? Is there any way out?*

It was in San Francisco, February 2, 1989. I was scheduled to speak that day at a huge conference where all the other speakers were far more experienced than I. Each of them was brilliant, witty, clever and inspiring. I had heard them all, and I knew I was way out of my league.

Somehow, I had convinced the conference meeting planners that I could do this—now I was convinced that I could *not!* Fear clutched at my throat as I glanced at the bedside clock and real-

ized that in only a few hours I was expected to appear poised, perky, prepared and polished before a
large audience.

The speech I had written, rehearsed and honed
to perfection seemed suddenly stupid and mun-
dane. My spiffy red "power" suit, hanging ready
for me on the closet door, wasn't sharp and busi-
nesslike anymore. In my panic-stricken eyes, it
now looked frumpy and dumpy.

"I can't do this!" I shouted at the bathroom mirror. "I don't even want to try!" I threw myself on
the bed, tears falling on the stiff white pillowcase.
"Oh, Lord, please help me out of this!" I cried.

A few minutes later I sat up and noticed beside
me, on the bedside stand, a little booklet I had carried with me for a few weeks but hadn't read. It
was titled *Thought Conditioners* by Norman Vincent Peale. Every page contained two short, powerful passages from Scripture, each followed by
two or three paragraphs of additional encouragement by Dr. Peale.

I didn't have to read beyond page one. The first
passage from Scripture read, "Peace I leave with
you, my peace I give unto you: not as the world
giveth, give I unto you. Let not your heart be
troubled, neither let it be afraid" (John 14:27,
KJV).

Dr. Peale's suggestion under those words was
that one should "sit quietly and allow these words
to pass unhindered through your thoughts. Con-
ceive of them as spreading a healing balm
throughout your mind."

The second Bible verse on page one was: "The things which are impossible with men are possible with God" (Luke 18:27, KJV). Dr. Peale followed that statement with the advice. "Pray about your problem. Keep relaxed. Don't worry. Avoid getting panicky. Never think, 'This can't be done.' Declare, 'It *can* be done; it is being done because God is doing it through me.' "[1]

The words were so perfect for my situation and the emotions I had been feeling that I could hardly believe it. I read the whole page again. Amazing! Incredible! I suddenly felt like laughing and singing: "Yes, yes, I *can* do this because God is doing it through me! Oh, thank you, Lord!"

I continued to repeat those wonderful verses as I showered and shampooed my hair. I sang my "Thank you, Lord" song as I applied my makeup and put on my spiffy red suit. I muttered the verses as I ate my quick breakfast of fruit, assembled my notes and strode confidently down the hall to the auditorium.

Later that evening, the resounding applause following my speech still ringing in my ears, I thanked God from my heart. As I look back now, I know that was the turning point in my speaking and writing career. I had been almost ready to hang it up, but from that day forward I have had faith in myself and faith that God would never let me down.

Back in my hotel room that night, I penned a sincere note of thanks to Dr. Peale. I had already heard the loving response from God, but I was surprised, a few days later, to receive also a loving response from Dr. Peale. His encouraging personal letter was the start of a now-and-then correspondence between us that lasted until his death in 1993. Dr. Peale's wife, Ruth Stafford Peale, has corresponded with me since that time, continuing her late husband's warm encouragement of my writing and speaking.

It's amazing to me how beautifully God answers prayer when we remember to stop fretting, stop moaning and groaning about our fears and problems and just get back to *trusting* Him and *asking* for His help.

I'll always be grateful that Dr. Peale, through his booklet, reminded me to do that; and that God, through His Word (and His Spirit), continues to remind me every day.

Note

[1] Norman Vincent Peale, *Thought Conditioners* (Pawling, NY: Foundation for Christian Living, 1977), 5.

Be anxious for nothing, but in everything by prayer and supplication, with thanksgiving, let your requests be made known to God; and the peace of God, which surpasses all understanding, will guard your hearts and minds through Christ Jesus. (Philippians 4:6-7, NKJV)

Diana L. James' articles and stories have appeared in several national magazines, numerous local and regional publications and in seven anthology books. She is editor/compiler of her own book, *Bounce Back* (Horizon Books, 1997), to which this book is a companion. Diana hosted a TV interview program for five years. She was a member of National Speakers Association for five years. She has been on the staff of CLASS (Christian Leaders, Authors and Speakers Seminars) for nine years and speaks for churches, retreats, women's conferences and bereavement groups. E-mail her at DianaJames@aol.com

Chapter 2

Attitude: The Life Conditioner

Therefore if any man be in Christ, he is a new creature: old things are passed away: behold, all things are become new. (2 Corinthians 5:17, KJV)

Seeds of Peace

Max Lucado

*W*ant to see a miracle? Try this. Take a seed the size of a freckle. Put it under several inches of dirt. Give it enough water, light and fertilizer. And get ready. A mountain will be moved. It doesn't matter that the ground is a zillion times the weight of the seed. The seed will push it back.

As far as I know, James, the epistle writer, wasn't a farmer. But he knew the power of a seed sown in fertile soil.

"Those who are peacemakers will plant seeds of peace and reap a harvest of goodness" (James 3:18, TLB).

The principle for peace is the same as the principle for crops: Never underestimate the power of a seed.

The story of Heinz is a good example. Europe, 1934. Hitler's plague of anti-Semitism was infecting a continent. Some would escape it. Some

would die from it. But eleven-year-old Heinz
would learn from it. He would learn the power of
sowing seeds of peace.

Heinz was a Jew. The Bavarian village of Furth,
where Heinz lived, was being overrun by Hitler's
young thugs. Tension mounted on the streets.

Hitler youth roamed the neighborhoods looking
for trouble. Young Heinz learned to keep his eyes
open. When he saw a band of troublemakers, he
would step to the other side of the street. Sometimes he would escape a fight—sometimes not.

One day, in 1934, a pivotal confrontation occurred. Heinz found himself face-to-face with a
Hitler bully. A beating appeared inevitable. This
time, however, he walked away unhurt—not because of what he did, but because of what he said.
He didn't fight back; he spoke up. He convinced
the troublemaker that a fight was not necessary.
His words kept battle at bay.

And Heinz saw firsthand how the tongue can
create peace. He learned the skill of using words
to avoid conflict. And for a young Jew in Hitler-
ridden Europe, that skill had many opportunities
to be honed.

Heinz's family escaped from Bavaria and made
their way to America. Later in life, he would
downplay the impact those adolescent experiences
had on his development.

But one has to wonder. For after Heinz grew up,
his name became synonymous with peace negotia-
tions. His legacy became that of a bridge builder.
Somewhere he had learned the power of the prop-

erly placed word of peace. And one has to wonder if his training didn't come on the streets of Bavaria.

You don't know him as Heinz. You know him by his Anglicized name, Henry. Henry Kissinger.[1]

Never underestimate the power of a seed.

You may not be called on to ward off international conflict, but you will have opportunities to do something more vital: to bring inner peace to troubled hearts.

Jesus modeled this. We don't see Him settling many disputes or negotiating conflicts. But we do see Him cultivating inward harmony through acts of love: washing the feet of men He knew would betray Him, having lunch with a corrupt tax official, honoring the sinful woman whom society had scorned. He built bridges by healing hurts. He prevented conflict by touching the interior. He cultivated harmony by sowing seeds of peace in fertile hearts.

Pause for a moment and think about the people who make up your world. Take a stroll through the gallery of faces that are significant to you. Mentally flip through the scrapbook of snapshots. Can you see their faces? Your spouse. Your best friend. Your kids. Your aunt across the country. Your neighbor across the street. Freeze-frame those mental images for a moment while I tell you how some of them are feeling.

I went to our family doctor not long ago, my first checkup since the one required for high school football seventeen years ago. Since I was way overdue, I ordered the works. One nurse put

me on a table and stuck little cold suction cups to
my chest. Another nurse wrapped a band around
my arm and squeezed a black bulb until my arm
tingled. Then they pricked my finger (which always hurts) and told me to fill up a cup (which is
always awkward). Then, with all the preliminaries
done, they put me in a room and told me to take
off my shirt and wait for the doctor.

There is something about being poked, pushed,
measured and drained that makes you feel like a
head of lettuce in the produce department. I sat on
a tiny stool and stared at the wall.

May I tell you something you know, but may
have forgotten? Somebody in your world feels like I
felt in that office. Someone in your gallery of people
is sitting on a cold aluminum stool of insecurity,
clutching the backside of a hospital gown for fear of
exposing what little pride he or she has left. And
that person desperately needs a word of peace.

Someone needs you to do for them what Dr.
Jim did for me.

Jim is a small-town doctor in a big city. And
though you know he's busy, he makes you feel
you are his only patient.

After a bit of small talk and a few questions
about my medical history, he put down my file
and said, "Let me take off my doctor hat for a
minute and talk to you as a friend."

He asked me about my family. He asked me
about my workload. He asked me about my stress.
He told me he thought I was doing a good job at
the church and that he loved to read my books.

After those few minutes, Dr. Jim went about his task of tapping my knee with his rubber hammer, staring down my throat, looking in my ears and listening to my chest. When he was all done, as I was buttoning up my shirt, he took his doctor hat off again and reminded me not to carry the world on my shoulders. "And be sure to love your wife and hug those kids, because when it all boils down to it, you're not much without them."

"Thanks, Jim," I said.

And he walked out as quickly as he'd come in—a seed sower in a physician's smock.

Want to see a miracle? Plant a word of love heart-deep in a person's life. Nurture it with a smile and a prayer, and watch what happens.

Don't forget the principle. Never underestimate the power of a seed.

Note

[1] Paul Harvey, *Paul Harvey's The Rest of the Story* (New York, NY: Bantam, 1977), 49.

Max Lucado is minister of the Oak Hills Church in San Antonio, Texas. He has written several best-selling books including: *In the Eye of the Storm, He Still Moves Stones, When God Whispers Your Name* and *A Gentle Thunder.* Max Lucado believes that the Beatitudes provide all that we need to discover the joy of God—but this requires a radical reconstruction of the heart. He communicates his beliefs each day on his national radio program, *Up Words*.

The Nurse
and the Mountain

Shirley Doan

She was a tall, pretty woman in her early forties, a real "head turner" with dark, thick hair, lovely skin. She was tired and eager to go home to bed and it showed in the circles under her eyes. *Thirty-two miles to go,* she sighed. It was an icy October night in Denver, Colorado. Kathy Chambers was coming back from one of the Denver hospitals where she worked as part of her nurse's training. She had been at the hospital since 2 p.m., working with a patient. She had risen at 5 a.m. to study and prepare for that clinical experience.

As Kathy drove, she reflected on her dream of becoming a nurse. It had been a hard decision, one that she and Jim, her husband of twenty-three years, had frequently discussed late into the night. They considered the added stress school and homework would bring, especially since she had been a homemaker for so many years while raising their five children.

Well, she thought now as she drove along, *nursing school has been a good experience, and I'm two-thirds finished! Soon I'll be a registered nurse.*

A tiny, knowing smile appeared as she remembered her first year of nursing school. She had passed the classes with good grades—all but one, that is. She did not pass the pharmacy course! The school officials told her that if she wanted to stay in school, she would have to take the whole first year over and pass pharmacy.

Many students would have dropped out at that time, but Kathy, after many prayers, decided not to quit. Taking that year over again was a mortifying experience, but she got through it and received a high grade in pharmacy as a result of studying harder than ever. Climbing this mountain was just one of the hurdles she had to overcome during her three years at nursing school.

Suddenly, without warning, an even larger mountain appeared, bringing even more devastating hurdles into Kathy's life. As she approached an intersection to enter the freeway, Kathy remembered she had not fastened her seat belt. She slowed down and reached up to grab the belt. Then she noticed police cars and policemen clearing an accident.

The next thing Kathy remembered, she was in the passenger seat. Her face was badly cut; there was blood everywhere and she could not see.

She felt intense pain all over her body. She became aware of voices outside the car. Realizing she needed help, she reached up to knock on the window, but there was no glass. She wanted to tell someone to get her purse, as it had information and they could call Jim. She passed out again, and when she regained consciousness she heard them prying her car door open. (She was told later that her car had been hit by a car driven by a drunk woman.)

The next time Kathy came to, she realized she was in an ambulance. *God, help me,* she prayed, *I'm seriously hurt.* They took her to a nearby hospital's trauma center where her head injury could be treated.

The next voice she heard was Jim's. She held out her hand. Jim came closer and took her hand in his. Kathy breathed a sigh of relief. *Thank God Jim's here. Now everything will be OK.* At last, she felt her body relax.

The hours passed and Kathy kept drifting in and out of a pain-soaked fog. She heard the doctors and Jim talking about doing a lavage—a procedure check for internal bleeding. They thought she had a ruptured liver.

They found no internal bleeding; but she had a concussion, fractures to her right facial bone, nerve damage in her face, three broken ribs, multiple contusions on her body from cut glass and a sprained left wrist.

Kathy was in the hospital for four-and-a-half days. Jim phoned the administrators of the nursing school to inform them of the accident and its severity. They told Jim that if Kathy missed more than one week of school, she would have to drop out and start all over. Also, they could not guarantee that she would be accepted back into the school.

"We can't show any favoritism," Jim was told. "We'll just remove her name from our active files."

"Please don't do that," Jim begged. "You don't know my wife." When Kathy learned of the comments of the nursing school administrators, she was upset and hurt. Worst was the thought of having to reapply for a program for which she had already sacrificed three years of her life. It was humiliating! She also felt angry, knowing she was being professionally trained for compassionate service to help the sick and dying, and yet the very system that was training her was treating her in a way that seemed hypocritical, insensitive and cold.

At this low point, Kathy found the courage and strength to climb yet another mountain. She knew she could never climb this mountain alone. Again and again she turned to God, praying fervently for guidance and strength.

Only one day after she was released from the hospital (a Monday morning) Kathy had to take a test at the nursing school. She was unable to focus her eyes to study for more than ten minutes at a time, but fortunately her classmates came through for her by lending her their audio tapes of the test notes.

Kathy drove herself to the school that Monday morning and walked to the office to get a temporary disability pass so she could park in the disability section of the parking lot. She then walked to the test center.

She entered the room wearing large sunglasses, because her face was badly bruised and swollen. She removed the sunglasses as she spoke to the woman who handed out the test papers. She explained about the accident and told her she would need more time than the normal fifty minutes to take the test.

The woman seemed amazed that Kathy was there. She patted her hand and told her to take as long as necessary. In addition to her painfully bruised face, her broken ribs hurt and she had a constant headache from the concussion.

She sat down with the test papers before her, not dwelling on passing, but looking for a method to focus on the papers. She noticed she became very dizzy trying to read the test paper when it was lying on the desk, so she held the paper up to eye level, read the question, then closed her eyes and thought about the answer.

Trying not to bend her head down too much, as it made her nauseous, she would then write the answer. She answered each question in this manner and finished about an hour and a half later.

Kathy knew she had reached the other side of the mountain when she later received word that she had gotten an A on this test.

The next several weeks at school were hard

physically and mentally. Kathy was so ill that many times she had to go to the bathroom to vomit, then go back to class and pretend nothing was wrong.

Kathy finished nursing school—and made the honor roll! She now has a job she loves in a Denver hospital. Besides setting an example in tenacity and courage for her family, she learned something about herself. She found that she was more than she thought she could be. She has moved a long way toward what many people are looking for—sometimes called inner harmony. Kathy knows who she is, in whom she believes, what she wants in life and where she is going afterward.

In Colorado they're still proud of the Rocky Mountains, the cowboys and a gutsy nurse named Kathy Chambers.

I can do all things through Christ who strengthens me. (Philippians 4:13, NKJV)

Shirley Randall Doan is a contributing writer for the *Julian News*, a weekly newspaper in Julian, California, her hometown. "The Nurse and the Mountain" is a true experience of her daughter, Kathy. Phone is (760) 765-2679. E-mail address is shirleyd@abac.com

Breakthrough to Joy

C. Christopher Knippers, Ph.D.

erhaps it's the balmy breezes, the mountains soaring straight to heaven out of the flat desert floor; perhaps it's the relaxed, friendly people and atmosphere; or perhaps it is all these that give Palm Springs, California the magical, exhilarating atmosphere that draws people from all over the world.

I had never considered Palm Springs as a possibility for anything more than a weekend getaway. Yet, there I was, leaving an exciting beach community that had been my home for almost twenty-three years to move to Palm Springs in the middle of summer—a time when the locals generally leave for the beach.

I had been in a fulfilling psychology practice on the beautiful grounds of a Christian conference center for fourteen years. My office was in a 100-year-old classic Southern California Mission-style hacienda. The seminars given at this Christian conference center gave me a chance to practice my love of working with groups of people.

My friends, as well as my niece and her family, were all fun to be with and were convenient for me to see anytime I wanted to. I walked the beach, went boating and attended plays, operas and concerts as part of my routine lifestyle. Why would I want to leave all of that?! And yet, that was actually part of the problem.

I discovered that I was subtly becoming the type of person I don't like to be around. I was becoming a little spoiled, inflexible, narrow and soft. I dined at fine restaurants every day, surrounded myself with beautiful environments and (mostly) perfect weather; my friends, colleagues and clients were all intelligent, sophisticated and successful white people; and my vacations were spent in the San Juan Islands where my family lives. (Do I sound a little like "Frazier"?)

I needed a change from my comfortable ruts. I wanted more variety in people, places and weather. I wanted to have to adapt to someone else's culture and values. I wanted to learn to appreciate more down-to-earth activities. I wanted to experience environmental extremes.

I met an amazing man named Dr. William Heard, a psychologist. We shared the same style of practicing psychotherapy, based upon the works of Martin Buber, author of *I and Thou* (Charles Scribner's Sons, 1958). Dr. Heard asked me to conduct a workshop one day a week in the Palm Springs area to teach lay counselors from churches and other nonprofit organizations how to practice counseling in a way that would maximize the power of God in the relationship (i.e., how to have an "I-Thou" relationship).

I decided to make the two-hour drive over the mountains one day each week to conduct the training. For several years, I had been wanting to devote more of my career to speaking and training. This seemed like the perfect opportunity.

It changed my life. People of many different cultures, races and socioeconomic backgrounds poured in to receive training in how to bring the power of God to all of their relationships. These diverse groups of people, with their diverse beliefs and lifestyles, all interacted and worked together in a spirit of love and understanding. People's lives were transformed before my eyes. Hopeless alcoholics were reconciling with their wives and children; sad, lonely single mothers were finding self-esteem and a renewed sense of purpose; and teenagers were spreading God's love to gang members.

The demand for the training increased phenomenally. The program was promised additional funding and staff to increase the number of workshops. There was enough work for me to do so that I could actually move to the desert and devote my time to this program. After months of prayer, I made the difficult decision to uproot my life and move to Palm Springs.

My decision upset many people who were dependent upon me, personally or professionally. It was painful to leave my comfortable life and the people I loved being with every day. But there I was, dismantling my life, packing up and moving to the desert.

After I came back in from helping the movers get the last load on the truck, the phone rang. It was one of the sponsors of the lay counselor training program. He had lost the support for additional trainings and was back to one day a week. He hoped it wouldn't "inconvenience" me.

My head was reeling. I hurled angry questions at myself: *How could you have made such a stupid misjudgment? Where did you go wrong in calculating the situation? Look at the years of struggle you threw away; look at the lives you've upset; how can you possibly put this move in reverse?* Nevertheless, though I was a bit numb, I decided to go ahead with the move. So I headed for Palm Springs.

I was comforted by the fact that a university in the desert area had asked me to teach a class, and it would be starting in a few weeks. I could teach the university class one day a week and conduct the lay counselor training one day a week. Those two jobs might get me by until I could think of something else.

The day after the move, I received another phone call. This time it was the university. The class that I was to teach had been canceled. Then that night I checked messages on my answering machine. There was one message from that morning which I had somehow overlooked. The director of the training program had called to tell me that the lay counselor training program was going to be canceled, entirely, due to a bizarre technical glitch.

For the next three weeks, I was in states of anger, confusion, self-recrimination and, at times, despair. Here I was in the middle of the desert in the intense heat with no friends, no family and almost no career. I felt negative and unhappy, which was certainly uncharacteristic of a man who for years had been described as one with a "healing" and "refreshing" presence.

I made a brief trip to my old haunts to visit a friend who lives at the beach. As I prepared to drive back to Palm Springs, dread came over me. I suddenly realized that I was heading back to a hot, lonely place that held virtually nothing for me. As I contemplated what I had given up in my life, my anger began to seethe and grow.

Just as I was pulling out of my friend's driveway, something caught my eye. I saw a pizza delivery man who appeared to be a robust man around thirty-five years old. He was about twenty feet away, and as I glanced at him he looked at me with a broad smile and a happy glow in his eyes, an expression that I knew could have come only from joy within.

In that instant, as I pulled out of the driveway and drove down the street, my anger disappeared. I sensed God saying to me, "Did you see that man? Did you see how genuinely happy he is? A healthy young man in his thirties is grateful to be delivering pizza and spreading joy to people, even to someone as angry as you. Do you think that there are some good things in your life on which you could focus, things for which you can be grateful—right now?"

All the way over the mountains, for two solid hours, I thought of things for which I could be grateful in my life, right then! By the time I arrived home, I felt better than I had felt in years! I pledged to myself and to God that I would continue to be sincerely grateful for every blessing in my life.

I have always avoided saying things like "count your blessings" to other people going through bad times. Somehow it seems like an easy brush-off, a discounting of their problem. I've said, "Count your blessings" many times to myself; but I would want to knock anyone's block off if he said it to me. (I still don't recommend saying it.) But there was something different about the pizza man's silent witness to me. It did not come as a judgment of my attitude, nor as a discounting of my feelings. His witness was simply from his soul to my soul. His was a witness of joy and thankfulness. I determined to follow his example.

The following week things began happening. I was asked to do ongoing lay counselor training for another program in the desert region. Another organization contracted me to train their staff in personal development, the university scheduled me to teach, and the program for which I had originally moved to the desert continued to operate after all, and even expanded! I'm enjoying a variety of cultures, and I've certainly learned to adapt to a season of less-than-perfect weather! I'm toughening up!

I know now that becoming truly thankful and joyful made it possible for me to be open to these opportunities and to gain the most from them. I now realize that no matter what kind of life we have or how much we have in life, we can never be truly happy until we humble ourselves in gratitude and learn to enjoy sincerely whatever blessings we can find, even in our darkest moments.

I have learned, in whatsoever state I am, therewith to be content. (Philippians 4:11, KJV)

 C. Christopher Knippers, Ph.D. in clinical psychology, is a psychotherapist with over twenty years' experience helping individuals and couples find fulfillment and peace of mind. Author of *Common Sense, Intuition, and God's Guidance,* Dr. Knippers also presents workshops and keynote speeches for audiences across the U.S. He has served as chairperson of the Mental Health Professional Network and as Education Director for Cancer Conquerors Foundation. He resides in Palm Springs, California. Contact him at (760) 416-3516.

Overload

Emilie Barnes

*D*o you have the type of home where nothing seems to get done? Where each room would take a bulldozer just to clean up the mess? You rush around all day never completing any one job, or if you do complete a task, there is a little one behind you, pulling and messing everything up again! There isn't one of us who hasn't experienced these feelings.

When I was twenty our baby daughter Jennifer was six months old. We then took in my brother's three children and within a few months I became pregnant. That gave Bob and me five children under five years old. My life was work, work, work—and yet I never seemed to get anywhere. I was running on a treadmill that never stopped and never moved ahead. I was always tired and never seemed to get enough done, let alone get enough sleep. I was fragmented, totally confused and stressed.

Then one day during my rushed quiet time with the Lord I read Proverbs 3:6: "In all your ways acknowledge him, and he will make your paths straight." I fell to my knees and prayed, "Please, God, direct my path. I acknowledge You to help me, Lord I'm going to allow You to lead me and not lead myself in my power. I want Your power and direction. Lord, I'm tired. I'm on overload with husband, home, children and meals. Please help me to put it all together and make it work to glorify You and Your children. Amen."

The Lord not only heard my prayer that day, but He honored it as well. I began a program that changed my life. I committed fifteen minutes (at least) per day to my quiet time with the Lord. I got up earlier each morning. The house was quiet, and my Lord and I talked as I read His Word and prayed.

Next I committed fifteen minutes each day to the organization of our home, concentrating on things I never seemed to get done: the silverware drawer, refrigerator, hall closets, photos, bookshelves, piles of papers. I committed to this for thirty days, and the pattern was set. God was directing my path. Our home changed dramatically. The cloud of homemaking stress lifted, and I had new direction. The Lord redeemed my time with Him. I had more time to plan meals, make new recipes, play with the children, take walks to the park, even catch a nap from time to time.

Looking back now as a grandparent, I can truly understand the meaning of acknowledging Him in all my ways. It's looking to God for help in all the ways of our life—our families, home, finances, commitments and careers. God gives us a promise: "I will direct your path."

Father God, sometimes I feel my life is truly on overload. There are days I am confused, frustrated and misdirected. I come to You on my knees, seeking Your undying patience and the hope You so graciously give. I ask for Your direction in my life. Make order out of disorder. Thank You. Amen.

Thoughts for action:
- Acknowledge Him today.
- Allow Him to direct your path.
- Commit to fifteen minutes today to clean something up.

Excerpted from 15 Minutes Alone with God, *Emilie Barnes, Copyright 1994, Harvest House Publishers, Eugene, Oregon. Used by permission.*

In all your ways acknowledge Him, and He shall direct your paths. (Proverbs 3:6, NKJV)

 Emilie Barnes has written over twenty-two books and coauthored six cookbooks. As an inspirational and practical speaker, she travels widely and shares her creative ideas on national radio and television programs. She and her husband Bob work together in their ministry, *More Hours in My Day*, which is also the title of one of her most popular books. She lives in Riverside, California.

Are You Ready for a Great Day?

Cassandra Woods

"Come on, guys, it's time to go." That statement has ended a flurry of activity on many mornings in my home. When the kids were five and six we'd grab up the book bags and lunch boxes and head for the car. It was time for school. As we climbed into the car, they hurried to get their seat belts on and got ready for what had become a tradition.

You see, nearly every morning we said a little chant. I would start it off by my saying, "Are you ready for a great day?"

"Hooray!" they would respond together.

"Are you ready for a great day?" I'd ask a little louder.

"Hooray!" they'd respond, a little louder.

Finally, shouting like a drill sergeant, I'd yell, "Are you ready for a greaaat day?"

With all the excitement a kindergartner and first-grader could muster, they'd shout, "Hoooo-Raaaay!" By that time our adrenaline was racing and we were all expecting a wonderful day.

Somewhere I'd heard that if you can get kids started on a positive note in the morning, they were more likely to have a good day. This attitude was typical for me. In the several months preceding this time, I devoured self-help books. I was looking for ways to make myself better. I was on a mission to become the world's best wife, mother, daughter, friend and Christian.

In my striving to be the perfect mom, I felt guilty if I wasn't with my child twenty-four hours each day. I baked cookies and volunteered at school. To be a perfect wife I struggled to keep a clean home, cook delicious meals and work at the family business.

To be a friend I felt I needed to be a listener whenever anyone needed an ear, and a server whenever someone was sick. I tried to be Super-woman. There was one problem: the needs of others were endless. I thought being a good Christian meant that I must smile all the time, help everyone in need and never have a problem of my own. That mind-set finally started me on a downward spiral.

I was demanding so much of myself that I could not physically or emotionally supply it all. The stress and pressure took their toll on me. Day after day, the tasks that I had once done easily became extremely difficult to complete. My thoughts seemed like they had to drag through molasses, and I just wanted to be alone.

Finally one morning when I'd gotten up to see the kids off to school—I wished I could stay in bed instead. I didn't want to have to deal with anything that day. As I forced a smile and said good-bye, my son's brown eyes seemed to connect with mine, and with joyful innocence he asked, "Mom, are you ready for a great day?" A little stunned, I replied in a weak voice, "Hooray."

At that moment a tradition I'd started, hoping to help them have a great day, boomeranged right back into my face. My son didn't know my inner struggle, but God used his words to challenge me to have a great day. I knew I had to do whatever it took to overcome the blues.

I asked myself, *What is a good Christian, anyway? Who said I have to do all of these things to be pleasing to God?* I realized that I had been taking all suggestions from the self-help books and trying to build my life according to them.

Then I remembered Romans 12:2, "Do not be conformed to this world, but be transformed by the renewing of your mind, that you may prove what is that good and acceptable and perfect will of God" (NKJV). That was it. I had read that verse but I wasn't living it. I had been trying to build my life on the teachings of man.

From that point I resolved to concentrate on building my life strictly on the Word of God. I committed myself to learning more about God so

I could hear *His* voice and know *His* specific will for my life.

These days, I still sympathize with my friends, I still bake cookies and help out at school, but only as I am prompted by God to do so. My life is more balanced. I meditate on God's Word and His daily plan for my life. I am being transformed into who *He* wants me to be. As I follow *His* will for my life, I'm *always* ready for a great day.

Hooray!

 Cassandra Woods is an inspirational writer and speaker who has seen God's Word become real in her own life. She finds great joy in sharing God's love with other women and encouraging them to develop an intimate relationship with God. Cassandra is married and the mother of three children. Contact her at P.O. Box 13311, Birmingham, AL 35202.

Finding the Power to Keep Loving

Gary Smalley

I'll never forget the day I realized that my lack of connection with God was primarily the result of my own decision to remain angry. My main anger source was my expectation that people and my job would fit nicely within my battery pack, that they would provide me with energy, love and satisfaction.

On this particular day, I was casually reading a section of Scripture and my eyes stopped at a verse that seemed to scream this message at me: "If you remain angry with anyone, you'll lose your ability to walk in the light of God and thus the ability to know the love of God" [Matthew 5:22, author's paraphrase].

We try to fit friends and loved ones into our battery packs. We rely on one person or a group of folks to meet our needs for love, purpose, excitement, fulfillment, ego gratification. . . . And you know what happens? They eventually let us down because they are human.

This is what happened to me in my period of great discouragement after graduate school when I went to work in the field of counseling with a reputable religious organization. Not long after I joined the staff, I grew uncomfortable with what I saw. I felt that top administrators were involved in highly questionable activities.

Eventually I had so much anger toward some of my coworkers that there were days I couldn't make myself go to work. I would call in sick. I distanced myself from my family too. For instance, I couldn't bring myself to sit and eat with them. I hid myself away in a bedroom for days on end. Our kids were only three, seven and nine at the time, and they needed their daddy, but emotionally I couldn't be there for them.

My wife, Norma, grew concerned, not only for my health and the family's, but also for our finances when I started talking about resigning.

"But you can't do anything else," she said pragmatically. "You've been trained only in this kind of work."

Her words were like a bucket of ice water thrown into my face. It was painful to acknowledge. I had a graduate seminary degree. What good would it do me if I left the religious milieu? I had no skills I knew of that would get me a job outside the fold. "You're right," I had to admit.

Years later I came to realize that going through

that trial opened me to a new, deeper compassion for people who are hurting and discouraged. As a result of this crisis, I also made massive strides in my own spiritual journey. Today I'm actually grateful I walked through all that hurt and depression, because it was the main motivation leading me to discover a personal God.

There are many good reasons to forgive the wrongs of others, but the most rewarding is to use it in our spiritual journeys. Consider the words of what came to be known as the Lord's Prayer: "Forgive us our trespasses as we forgive those who trespass against us." This indicates His forgiveness of us is connected to our forgiveness of others.

I have talked about my crisis twenty years ago and what precipitated my feeling distant from God—how anger had blocked my relationship with God. I can briefly summarize the two main lessons I have learned that have made my journey more than worthwhile. These two truths were first planted in my heart during my college years. But in my midlife-crisis years they really took root, and they formed the essence of my faith in God. They are the soil that nurtures my marriage, my relationships with family and friends, and my work. But they didn't become personalized until after my discouragement.

These truths are captured in this quick summary of all the biblical laws: "Love God with your whole heart, and love others as you love yourself" [Matthew 22:37-39; Mark 12:30-31; Luke 10:27, author's paraphrase].

When I read that commandment as a college kid, I wondered, *What in the world does that mean— Love God?* It was embarrassing even to say it out loud. You can love your wife, your girlfriend, fishing or golf, but how do you love God? It seemed too strange. But it was a lifesaving truth I recalled in my depression, and then it began to make sense. I certainly don't know how God does it, but He somehow makes Himself real to those who wholeheartedly seek after Him. I'll try to explain this as I've come to understand it.

I came to realize that the word *love* is an action verb that indicates you're doing something for someone because that someone is valuable to you. It is closely connected to the word *honor*.

This word honor has helped me draw close to God. As I have established God as my highest value in life, God has miraculously reached out and made Himself real to me in many ways. I don't understand how He does this anymore than I understand how my computer works, yet I go on typing. . . . And in my spiritual life I still go on honoring and believing, and God continues to make His presence known to me.

I've learned that as I honor God, I learn to love God. As I set aside the anger that keeps me distant from Him, I am ushered into His presence; I am able to experience Him in my spirit.

I have hundreds of examples of how He has made Himself known to me. Many involve inner assurance—peace and comfort and wisdom—in the midst of crisis, a rejuvenating joy and an increased desire to love others. I didn't have to work at these things; they seemed to be given to me without effort on my part. All I did was draw closer to Him by honoring Him. As I honored Him, I got to know and trust Him.

When I no longer felt distanced from God, I could better love others (and myself). When I started increasing the value of others—honoring them—my desire to help them increased. As I treasured people, I loved them. I didn't have to work up a love for people, it just grew as I honored them more.

Excerpted and abridged from Making Love Last Forever, *Gary Smalley, Copyright 1996, Word Publishers, Nashville, Tennessee. All rights reserved.*

You shall love the Lord your God with all your heart, and with all your soul, and with all your strength, and with all your mind; and your neighbor as yourself. (Luke 10:27, RSV)

 Gary Smalley is an internationally known speaker on family relationships. He holds a seminary master's degree and a bachelor's degree in psychology. His books and videos have sold over 9 million copies, and he has been featured on hundreds of radio and television shows. He is president of Today's Family based in Branson, Missouri.

The Blessed Blizzard

Joyce A. Minatra

It was a cold, brittle winter day. The sky was brilliant blue and the snow, piled deep in the yard, glistened in the sun. I stood at the window washing dishes, tears dripping off my chin into the soapy dishwater. I felt trapped by the chaos of my home as well as the winter cold.

I had been a Christian only a short time, and it was as if the devil were pulling me down and down. I was drowning and only my nose was above the water. I clung to the Lord, my hand gripped in His, but it seemed I was slipping and couldn't get free from that downward slide. As the tears coursed down my cheeks, I silently cried out, *Lord help me, please help me.*

My ninety-two-year-old grandmother, Nanny, had been living with us for several months. Since we had no extra bedroom she slept in a front downstairs room open to the stairs leading to our upstairs bedrooms.

A sharp and observant woman, she commented on everything that went on in our household. She had never been a favorite of mine, and having her invade our personal and private lives stretched my nerves taut. I couldn't leave her by herself, and she heard every move I made during the day. When she didn't hear me she called out until I answered. This was so stressful that I even found myself hiding in the center of the living room out of her sight. I prayed for relief, for a way to care for Nanny and for my sanity.

Then the septic system backed up. In a house with six adults dependent on one bathroom, we had a big problem.

My daughter and my niece, who lived with us, were scurrying around getting ready to go to a basketball tournament out of town with the youth group of our church. Nanny was wandering about with a perplexed look, perhaps wondering what she was doing in this madhouse. My son Lee was home from the Coast Guard for the weekend, and he and my husband, Wayne, were attempting to find the blockage in our septic system. This meant dismantling pipes in the cellar as well as shoveling a path through the snow to the septic tank. Home had never felt so chaotic, smelled so foul or seemed so unhomey.

The telephone rang. It was a friend from the church asking if I would be able to drive some of the kids to the tournament in Maine. I asked Wayne, and very graciously he said, "Go." He would take care of Nanny and try to get things back in running order by the time I got back late that night. Since I would only be gone for the day, little preparation was necessary, and soon I was on my way, leaving Wayne, Lee and Nanny to fend for themselves.

The games went on into the evening with everyone screaming, cheering and rooting for their teams. I found myself caught up in the excitement, not giving a thought to what I had left behind at home. When the games were over and we were gathering our things for the trip home, someone shouted, "It's snowing!"

And so it was. A true blizzard had blown in; snow swirled and piled up in great drifts. The highways were closed. We couldn't go home.

We stayed in the church that had hosted the tournament. It was a quiet place and the lights were low. Several of the kids gathered around the piano and sang while others sat and chatted quietly. No one was sleepy. I went to the altar and knelt quietly before the Lord.

While the storm raged outside, the Lord was giving me peace on the inside. It was blessed, sweet communion time for the Lord and me. I don't know how long I stayed at the altar, but there was little sleep for me that night.

Morning dawned bright, crisp and windy—not a cloud in the sky. Great mounds of sparkling snow were the only evidence of the storm the night before. Roads had been plowed and were opened for travel. Within a few hours I was driving up the steep hill to our home.

As I rounded the sharp corner at the top of the hill, my car, instead of going around the corner, went into a soft, deep snowbank, burying the front of the car. We struggled out of the car and walked the rest of the way with the wintry wind biting and nipping at our cheeks.

When we walked in the door of our home, nothing had changed. Wayne was still working to unclog our septic system and get the bathroom functional. Lee had been called back to the Coast Guard because of the storm. Nanny was still wandering around confused. The odor in the house was still strong and unpleasant.

But one thing was different—I was changed. The Lord had rescued me from my despair and discouragement and given me peace. He showed me He will be with me through the storms of my life and He will never let me go. I knew that with His help and His strength I could handle the tasks before me. On that snowy night in the church I had learned a deeper meaning of the verse, "Be still, and know that I am God" (Psalm 46:10).

Joyce A. Minatra is a Bible study teacher and speaker for retreats and women's groups. She is the author of *When Parents Grow Old* and is presently working on her second book. She is on the staff of CLASS (Christian Leaders, Authors and Speakers Seminars, Inc.). She and her husband, Jack, now live in Burnet, Texas.

Chapter 3

Facing Fear and Failure

For God hath not given us the spirit of fear; but of power, and of love, and of a sound mind. (2 Timothy 1:7, KJV)

The Ability to Fail

Tim Hansel

Success is never final. Failure is never fatal. It is
courage that counts. —Winston Churchill

A young man had just been elected to take over as bank president. He strode into the outgoing bank president's office and said, "Sir, I would like your advice. What will make me as successful as you?"

The older man looked up from his papers, eyed the young man up and down and rather curtly said, "Two words: Good decisions!"

The young man thanked the outgoing president and left the office. But then he turned and knocked on the door and said, "Please forgive me for bothering you again, but how does a person know he's making good decisions?"

The bank president waited for a moment. Then, going back to his work, he said, "One word: Experience!"

The young man nodded and turned to walk out. But before he reached the door, he stopped and turned around.

"Yes?" said the outgoing president, putting the papers down again.

"Well," the young man asked, "how do I get that experience?"

"Two words," the other man answered. "Bad decisions!"

Bad decisions. Mistakes. Failure. We don't like to admit it, but we know the terms well.

Believe it or not, the ability to fail successfully is one of the most critical ingredients of living a lifestyle at our peak level. Failure may be the tap-root of our relationship with Jesus Christ. To become Christians, we have to admit we are failures. We can't make it on our own. We must admit to failure to gain an entrance exam into the kingdom.

Is it just a coincidence that the Bible is a rich tapestry of failure and faith? Psalm 23, that incredible statement of confidence and security, comes immediately after David's statement in Psalm 22 about how he had become scorned by man. In the midst of these awful feelings of failure David understood God's power, and then wrote the masterpiece of faith that touches us thousands of years later.

We are encouraged in James 5:16 to be in the habit of admitting our sins to each other and praying for each other. The fact that we conceal our failures from one another almost made me give up on myself as a Christian.

My life includes a long list of failures. I've kidded with some people that I didn't even become a Christian in the "right" way. As I mentioned before, I'm one of those Christians who doesn't know the exact time and place or even the moment when I became a Christian. I struggled, doubted and at times simply refused to allow God's grace to change me. My conversion, though real enough, was a long, drawn-out process that lasted over a period of years. I feel like C.S. Lewis, who said he was dragged "kicking and screaming" into the kingdom.

When I first became a Christian, I found my wild behavior somewhat hard to break. My philosophy of life at that time would be best described as "somewhere to the left of Whoopee." I had a difficult time steering my life in a new direction.

What made it even worse was the fact that other Christians around me were either unable or unwilling to share their failures and struggles with me. I became convinced that I was the only one who didn't have his act together. I was wrestling with immense guilt. After about a year of struggle, I came to the conclusion that God couldn't love me.

Fortunately, a dear friend, Don McClean, leveled with me about some of his problems. He told me about the personal temptations and struggles he had been battling for years—and some of them were exactly like my own. As this deeply spiritual man was talking, I realized that if *he* had these struggles, then maybe I wasn't hopeless after all. His "confession," his honest sharing, totally changed my life. To this day, I thank Don with all my heart. In fact, my oldest son's middle name is McClean, in honor of this man who so changed my life with his honesty and compassion.

I'll never forget something my college landlady said to me. I asked her, "Mrs. Dingler, if my 'old self' is crucified with Christ, why is it still wiggling?"

She gave me this gentle smile and said, "Tim, you've got to remember that crucifixion is a slow death."

I'm continually amazed with my own failures. But the wonder of it all is that God keeps working on me and through me anyway. I'm convinced He's worked more through my failures than my successes. I'm so grateful the Bible is packed with failures who became champions of the faith. Their stories show me that God isn't looking at our achievements, but at us—and that even my failures can be used for His ultimate glory.

Excerpted and abridged from Holy Sweat, *Tim Hansel, Copyright 1987, Word Publishers, Nashville, Tennessee. All rights reserved.*

My flesh and my heart may fail, but God is the strength of my heart and my portion forever. (Psalm 73:26)

 Tim Hansel was raised in Seattle, Washington and is a graduate of Stanford University. He has written four books and founded Summit Expedition, a wilderness ministry with life-changing impact (including special programs for handicapped and delinquent youths). A popular conference speaker, Tim and his family live in LaVerne, California.

The Perfect Size

Paula Mitchell

"*W*ow! You look thin in that dress! You should wear dresses like that all the time."

I bought the dress for the color, the lines and the fabric. But most of all because I feel pretty in it. I really believe *that's* the reason I look good in the dress—why should it come down to size and weight? For thirty years I had allowed the numbers on a scale to rule my life. But never again!

As a child I was tall and gangly. I could eat anything and everything and still fit the mold my parents had for me. The summer before eighth grade marked the beginning of my struggle with weight—I ballooned up to the weight of 130 pounds. Too much, too fast. I was put on a clothes budget of two dresses, two skirts and two blouses.

"You will wear *only* these clothes," my parents told me, "until you get down to the weight you should be. If you had any self-control, self-respect or self-discipline, this wouldn't be so difficult."

It was useless to argue. I was in junior high, blossoming into a woman's body, and on a diet. I was pretty sure I had self-control and self-respect, but like many thirteen-year-olds, I didn't have a lot of self-discipline.

Bulimia was not well-known or publicized during the early '60s. Bingeing and purging were not subjects written about or discussed. However, the magazines were filled with articles on being slim, well-groomed and popular. Those articles and the pictures of slim, trim girls reaffirmed my mother's words, "You don't want to look like you have let yourself go."

By the time I entered the ninth grade I was the "proper" size and rewarded by new clothes, compliments and words of praise. Little did anyone know that I was bingeing during the day and purging each night. On the outside I was just what everyone wanted, but on the inside I was empty; in fact, I kept emptying myself each night.

My weight stabilized during my high school years. Bingeing and purging episodes were fairly well controlled, usually occurring only after pizza parties and other food-oriented social events.

Why can everyone else eat but I can't? I asked myself. Perhaps my mother was right. Perhaps I didn't have any self-control or self-discipline. My self-respect was certainly low. The worse I felt about myself, the more I ate. The more I ate, the more I purged. The more I purged, the worse I felt about myself. Down, down, down the cycle went.

After my first child was born, I knew I had to get back into shape. I was not going to be one of those women who "let herself go" after having a baby. I whipped myself into shape. Once I got my figure back, I again received compliments and smiles. That was nice. I figured my weight-loss method wasn't too awful, considering the ovation I received. From the outside it seemed as if I had regained my self-control, self-respect and self-discipline—I was again a size ten.

But my love for cooking turned out to be a curse. Once I began cooking and baking, I began to gain weight. As the pounds became visible, the comments began again. "Aren't you starting to put on a bit of weight?" "Are you sure you want that cookie?" my husband would say.

"Don't become one of those fat housewives," my mother admonished.

Again the weight, again the purging. Appearance was all-important. It didn't seem to matter that I was caring for my family and volunteering for the Red Cross. What really mattered, according to the message I was receiving, was appearance. Size was of *utmost importance*.

By the time I was thirty-five, I had finally lost weight the old-fashioned way, by sensible eating and exercise. I had survived bulimia for twenty-three years. I thought I had it beaten.

I was also divorced. That year, as a single parent of two teenage sons, I worked three jobs, barely keeping body and soul together. But I was *THIN!* I thought I could keep the weight off this

time. I could put the purging behind me—along
with the shame and guilt.

But within three years I was purging again.
Each time I called my childhood home, one of the
first questions I got was, "So how is your weight,
Paula?" What a barometer to use in ascertaining a
person's emotional state! Yes, food had always
been my drug of choice; but why not ask how I
was feeling, rather than about my weight?

When I became larger than the size twelve my
new husband, Dick, had married, I was gripped
by fear. *Will he reject me?*

I reminded myself: *Weight was an issue in my first
marriage and divorce. Surely I can't let that happen
again!* Dick thought I had self-discipline and self-
esteem. By putting on all this weight, I was showing him I didn't really possess those qualities.

As I added depression to my list of shortcom-
ings, life became a vicious downward spiral again.
Once again, purging became a regular part of my
life. I was back to a laxative chaser with each meal.
Again the weight came off. Bulimia had won
again.

Who was that woman in the mirror? Oh, how I
hated her! She was such a fake—but she was *thin*.
But no matter how thin I was on the outside, I felt
fat on the inside.

Then one day in 1994, while I was praying,
the Lord showed me the person *He* saw: a lovely
and loving woman who has self-control and self-
discipline. He told me that without these two at-
tributes I would have gone through with my

suicidal thoughts. "It doesn't matter what size you are, Paula," the Lord told me. He thought I was perfect. How wonderful it was to be set free from the bondage of the past!

Once I submitted my will to Jesus, He guided me to become the person He saw. "Be not conformed to actuary numbers or Madison Avenue advertisements, but be transformed by the Spirit" became Paula's translation of Romans 12:2. Daily I seek that transformation. Daily I am blessed.

Today my closet is full of beautiful size sixteens and eighteens. When people ask me what size I wear, I reply: "Only the Lord knows. I shop for color and fit, not size." I am being truthful, for only the Lord Jesus knows my true size. You see, I fit perfectly into His world.

Paula Mitchell speaks and writes of her experiences, from her self-conscious teens, her marriage to an army officer, years of parenthood, single parenthood, remarriage, step-parenthood and finally, empty nest. She leaves her audiences with practical steps toward understanding God's love and His leading for their lives. Paula and her husband, Dick, live in western New York. E-mail: RBMCO@aol.com

He's Always There

Kathie Clarke

Help me! My mind was screaming for someone—anyone—to help me, but no one noticed, because the cry was within. Outwardly I was listening to a sermon that droned on and on. The sermon might have been good, but I couldn't concentrate on it. My mind kept returning to my circumstances. I felt so alone. I had just moved to the area and didn't know anyone well enough to confide in. This I did know: I needed help and needed it badly.

My marriage was coming apart. It wasn't supposed to be this way. I was a Christian. My marriage was supposed to last. My husband had started coming home later and later, and then a couple of nights he hadn't come home until morning. He wouldn't discuss it. I didn't know what was happening, but I felt panic rising.

I went home that day determined to do all I could do to salvage my marriage. I loved my husband, and my children needed their daddy.

I tried to "fix" things in every way I knew how. I prayed, I fasted, I tried to be the perfect wife. I also worried and fretted, trying to keep on being a good mother, trying to keep things normal at work and pretending that things were all right in my life when they were far from it.

One Saturday I was so tired and exhausted I lay down for a short nap. When I awoke, I realized that I didn't care if I ever got up again. A depression had entered my heart like a heavy weight that wouldn't let me go.

I lay there for a long time, and then two thoughts came to my mind and wouldn't leave. The first was, *I can't just keep on lying here. My children need me.* The second was: *This depression can't be from God, so I must fight it.* I thought of a verse that I had memorized years before: "For God did not give us a spirit of timidity, but a spirit of power, of love and of self-discipline" (2 Timothy 1:7).

I got up determined that I would not let the enemy take away my peace or my sound mind. I went to a psychiatrist on an emergency basis, and he gave me some antidepressant pills and told me to make an appointment on Monday. When I got home, I took the pills out and sat looking at them for a long time. Somehow I knew God had a different solution for me. I knew the Holy Spirit could heal my spirit. I decided to put the pills away and try it His way.

I found myself rehearsing in my mind all the

things I had tried to do to make my marriage work. After listing them, I realized that nothing was making the least bit of difference. In desperation I suddenly dropped to my knees and told the Lord, *I have done everything I can do. I give up. You can have the problem. I can't do any more.* Somehow, in that moment of total surrender, I gave God everything: my husband, my marriage and my ideas about what He should do about it all.

What happened next was a once-in-a-lifetime experience for me. I felt a blanket of peace come down from the sky and completely cover me. It felt wonderful. I felt light and free for the first time in months. I don't know how long I was there on my knees but when I got up I was a different person.

The next day people I knew looked at me and exclaimed, "What has happened that makes you so happy?" Actually, nothing about my circumstances had changed, but I was changed inside. The depression was totally gone and has never returned. I remember it now as a distant memory, a reminder of the fruitlessness of trying to work out my own life instead of leaving it with God.

I am not telling you this because I have discovered a secret formula for getting out of depression. Jesus isn't into formulas. Each of us is different. Circumstances for each of us are different. He helps each of us in different ways.

I have learned, and I know for sure, that when things are going very badly for you, when you can't go on any longer, you can still trust the

Lord. He cares. He is there for you. You, however, must make the decision to seek Him and
trust Him. If you do, things will turn out for the
good eventually, but probably not in the way you
expect.

Was there a storybook ending to my story? No
and yes. No, things did not end perfectly with
everyone living happily ever after. But yes, things
did end up for the best and I am happy and I am
still trusting Him. He has not failed me and He
cannot fail me because He is Love and He is always there.

*Cast your burden on the LORD, and he will sustain
you. (Psalm 55:22, RSV)*

 Kathie Clarke has had many ministries
including Sunday school teacher, Youth
For Christ leader, coleader of intercity
mission trips for teens with Youth With
A Mission, freelance writer, teacher for
twenty years in a Christian school, wife,
mother and grandmother. She feels that
all her talents come from God and should
be used for His kingdom. Contact her at Rt. 3, Box 99A2,
Tonganoxie, KS 66086.

To Overcome Fear– Just Do It!

Douglas A. Clark

During my lifetime I have faced—and conquered—three major fears. The first of these fears came during my childhood, the second during adolescence and the third persisted until the year before my retirement. Three brief words summarize these life-influencing fears: bees, people and water.

I believe I had good reason for the first fear, that of bees. During my early childhood I had two unfortunate experiences which formed the basis of this fear. I was helping my dog Teddy pull a groundhog out of a farmer's stone fence. In doing so I evidently disturbed a yellow jackets' nest, for suddenly they were swarming around me and stinging. I managed to outrun them, but long before I got out of their range, I developed a fear of being stung.

A second experience merely confirmed my

original fear. This time it was not yellow jackets, but large bumblebees. I was walking behind a neighbor's hay wagon when one of the wheels ran over the bumblebee's nest. The angry bees lit on me, and as I tried to brush them off my arms, neck and shirt, I was stung repeatedly.

Because of these painful childhood experiences, I developed an irrational fear of bees. It did no good for me to be told, "Leave them alone and they'll leave you alone." I knew better than that, or so I thought.

One warm summer day I was walking over to visit a neighbor and impulsively took a shortcut across a wide field of clover. I had forgotten about the bees until I suddenly became aware of their loud buzzing as they drew nectar from the clover blossoms. I stopped dead in my tracks and stood there, rooted to the ground in fear. I realized I was in the center of the field, and no matter which way I turned, there was no way I could escape brushing by the bees. I don't know how long I stood there, but finally with a fervent prayer, "Lord, help me," I walked rapidly out to the dirt road. When I reached the safety of the road it dawned upon me that I had not been stung by any of the bees. It was then I discovered my fear was gone.

My second fear was born during my early adolescence. It was the fear of people. I still do not understand what triggered this fear, but I know it was real. One experience still stands out vividly in my mind, for it had a devastating effect on me and prevented my peace of mind for several years. I was not afraid of individuals, but panicked when standing before a group.

A high school teacher assigned each student a topic to address briefly. After preparing it as best I could, I sat each day in class with my stomach in knots, hoping she would not call on me. But one afternoon I received the dreaded call: "Douglas, you're next."

Somehow I made my way to the front of the classroom and blurted out what I had planned to say. With a sigh of relief I began to return to my seat when the teacher said, "Douglas, I didn't understand a word you said." My terror was not yet over, for I had to repeat what I had said. I doubt if the second try was an improvement, but the teacher had mercy on me and let me take my seat at the back of the classroom.

Victory over this fear was finally achieved in college. A close friend of mine, Bob, was chosen head usher in the church I attended. The building was small, but always packed with college students, attracted by the sermons of the dynamic young student pastor. Several times Bob asked me to help take up the offering, but I always declined. I could not face the crowd.

One Sunday evening Bob caught me unawares, and I found myself at the front, head bowed, waiting for the pastor to finish his prayer of thanks. When the prayer concluded, I was handed an offering plate and turned, with my own silent prayer for help, to the first row. I glanced at the congregation, and to my surprise—and relief—found no one was paying any attention whatsoever to me. Again God proved to be faithful and merciful.

Gradually this fear subsided, and to this day I can testify that in a lifetime of preaching and teaching in university classrooms I have no fear of speaking to groups of any size.

My third and final fear to overcome was the fear of water. A well-meaning uncle decided that as a boy of eight I should know how to swim. The idea was fine, but the method of instruction was brutal. He took me by the hand out to where the water was deep enough to reach my chin, and then let go. "Swim back to shore," he said matter-of-factly.

My only problem was that I had no idea of how to go about it and quickly lost my balance and plunged in over my head. When I managed to get back on my feet a wave knocked me over again. I made it back to the beach, but I was now a frightened child who was afraid of the water.

This dread of the water prevented me from participating in the fun that boys my age experienced. No one ever made a serious attempt either to teach me to swim or to overcome my fear of attempting it.

At the age of sixty-four, a year from retirement, I finally overcame this fear and learned to swim. My wife Ruth and I were spending a summer in Belize, Central America, assisting a small mission church. We attended a mission conference on a key north of Belize City. The weather was hot and humid, and each afternoon we retreated to the cool ocean waters. There we stood, waist deep, and just talked together.

One day I confessed I was unable to swim. One missionary replied, "Why, I used to teach swimming. There's nothing to it. All you do is relax, take a deep breath, lie back in the water and let your feet float to the surface." *Sure*, I thought to myself, *that's easy for you to say. You have no idea how afraid I am of the water.*

Later, when no one was watching, I followed her instructions and was amazed to find my feet actually rising and my body floating. I then stretched out my arms and made motions which slowly propelled me along the dock. I was actually swimming! The fear disappeared, and while I am by no means an accomplished swimmer, I enjoy going into a pool or ocean and going in over my head without concern. From childhood to adolescence to retirement I have met and overcome, by God's grace, my three fears.

But thanks be to God! He gives us the victory through our Lord Jesus Christ. (1 Corinthians 15:57)

Douglas A. Clark is a "retired" pastor who has served as interim pastor on every continent except Antarctica and has visited eighty-seven countries so far. He has three sons and four grandchildren. His wife of forty-three years went to be with the Lord in 1987. He has continued to serve the ministry and has added writing to his accomplishments. He resides in Mesa, Arizona (when he's home).

Chapter 4

Healing Family Relationships

Dear friends, let us love one another, for love comes from God. . . . If we love one another, God lives in us and his love is made complete in us. (1 John 4:7, 12)

The Language of Love

Laura Sabin Riley

Although I grew up in a Christian home, I was a rebellious teenager. My parents did everything they knew to raise me according to God's standards. I rebelled anyway. Feeling I couldn't measure up to their high standards, I set my own. I went to college 500 miles from home and became involved in a lifestyle that was not pleasing to God. Then— still a teenager—I was in a car accident one night that could have ended my life.

It was my car, but I was in the passenger seat. The friend driving was intoxicated and lost control of the car on a winding, gravel mountain road. The car flipped end over end and slid down an embankment. I remember hearing the sounds of screeching tires, grinding metal, tinkling glass and my own screaming. The rollover sent me flying through the front windshield. I landed on the ground outside the car, my long blonde hair pinned between the roof of the car and the ground.

Lying on the ground outside the car, I shrieked, "Help me!" The three other teenagers in the car crawled out from the wreckage and freed me from underneath the car. An ambulance and the police arrived. The police officers said it was a miracle any of us were alive. We all walked away with only minor scrapes and bruises. The biggest bruise was on my heart.

I knew I had to contact my parents. I was not looking forward to telling them that I was in a car with a bunch of party-happy teenagers, myself included, and that as a result my car was now totaled. I sat on my bed in my dorm room for a long time, hand poised over the telephone, tears streaming down my face. I knew my parents would be incredibly disappointed. I was afraid to tell them how badly I had failed them.

Nervously, I picked up the phone and dialed. When my mother answered, I tried to talk, but instead, the only sound that came was the sound of me choking on my tears.

"Laura! What is it? What's wrong?" my mom said. "Whatever it is, just tell me. I'm your mother. I love you."

That made me cry even harder. "You may not love me after what I have to tell you," I blurted out.

"Of course I will," she said in a calm, soothing voice.

With both of my parents on the line now, I finally managed to tell them of the whole ordeal. Silence.

I winced as I waited for their anger to unleash

itself. I could hear the clock in my room ticking—I had never noticed it was so loud. I continued to wait. I heard my mom draw in a deep breath, and I subconsciously mimicked her. *Here it comes*, I thought.

Their response was not what I expected. They didn't lecture or scold. They told me they loved me. They also told me they were disappointed in the choices I had made in my lifestyle, but they reinforced their love for me. I had to live with the consequences of my actions and go without a car for the rest of the school year. But my behavior had not cut me off from their love.

I was so surprised and relieved by their instant affection for me that another stream of tears began to flow—tears of joy, not pain.

For the first time in my life, I understood the love of parents. Their love for me was not conditional, based on my performance or behavior. There was nothing I could do that would separate me from their love. They wouldn't always agree with my choices, especially if those choices were outside of God's will for my life, but they would love me all the same. Their words of love poured over me like a healing balm.

Through that incident, I began to grasp not only my parents' devotion to me, but also the unconditional love of my heavenly Father. I began to see Him not as a controlling God who wanted to dominate my life and take all of my fun away, but as a God who loved me whether I deserved it or not and only wanted what was best for me.

I began to turn my life back toward the behavior that I knew was pleasing to God and best for me. A transformation took place over the course of time, and I have learned to listen to God's voice and to seek Him in all that I do. I still make mistakes, but understanding His unconditional love and accepting the grace of His forgiveness has helped me to bounce back time and time again.

I look back on that accident as an event that catapulted me not only out the windshield, but into a new understanding of the love of my mother, my father and my heavenly Father.

For I am persuaded that neither death nor life, nor angels nor principalities nor powers, nor things present nor things to come, nor height nor depth, nor any other created thing, shall be able to separate us from the love of God which is in Christ Jesus our Lord. (Romans 8:38-39, NKJV)

In addition to being a wife and the mother of two active boys, Laura Sabin Riley is a freelance writer and speaker. She has published numerous short stories and articles and has recently completed her first book, *All Mothers Are Working Mothers*. It is scheduled to be released by Horizon Books in Spring 1999. Laura lives in Yuma, Arizona. E-mail: Rileys-Ranch@juno.com

The Lost Years

Marie Asner

By the time I was born, my father was an alcoholic. He celebrated the news of my mother's pregnancy after twelve years of marriage by getting drunk. He celebrated my birth by getting drunk. Any day, for any reason, he would get drunk. Amazingly, he was able to hold down a job.

My mother worked several jobs to pay for groceries and a baby-sitter. My father's salary went for the mortgage and car payments and his alcohol. As a teenager I began to do baby-sitting as a means of earning spending money for myself, and I held down a series of part-time jobs through high school and into college.

I couldn't depend on my father for anything. If he said he would be at a school function, he wouldn't show up. Eighth-grade graduation, high school graduation—he was never there. He was "working," which meant eight hours of work and then hours in a bar somewhere.

He embarrassed me so much the one time he did show up that I couldn't go to school the next day. It was an afternoon, fourth-grade children's program and my father's shift ended at noon. Instead of going home for lunch and changing clothes, he "drank lunch," then walked from the bar to the school, arriving after the program started. He fell over chairs finding a seat and caused such a commotion by pointing and yelling, "That's my daughter," that the principal had to usher him out, amid loud protestations and curses from my father. I was horrified and left the stage in tears when my classmates began to tease me.

My mother was a music teacher and church organist. She taught me to play the piano and then began sending me to other teachers for lessons in theory and the classics. By the time I was fourteen, I was a substitute organist for several churches in our area. How I wished and prayed that my father would see and hear me play the organ. Time after time I would look out at the congregation, hoping to see his face, but it never happened. In fact, because my mother worked so much, there was never a familiar face in the audience—only strangers.

There are many occasions for recitals and concerts when one is a music major. My mother and grandmother tried to attend them, and each time I would hesitantly say, "Could Dad come too?" To which one of them would reply, "Oh, he's probably going to be working then." Or, "He'll try to come, I'm sure he will." But of course he never showed up. I think many of my classmates thought my father was dead. He might as well have been.

Years passed and I was about to graduate with a music degree. I had continued organ substitution as a means of financial support while I was in college and found myself playing at my teachers' churches—at least then there would be someone I knew in the congregation. Near graduation time, my vocal music teacher asked me to play for a small wedding at her church.

The week of the wedding, I prayed a special prayer for the couple and then added, *God, all these years I've been praying for my father to hear me play. I'm putting it in Your hands now. I'm through wishing for myself. Your will be done.* I should have prayed that way years before, because I immediately felt a sense of relief.

That Saturday afternoon turned out to be a sunny day with fresh April breezes and the fragrance of lilacs in the air. *A special wedding day,* I thought as I entered the church. The prelude music I'd chosen seemed to be agreeable to the people near the organ and I could see satisfied smiles on their faces. After I'd finished the processional and the bride and groom were at the altar, I looked out at the entire congregation and almost lost my composure—there, at the back of the church, sat my father. I knew immediately he was sober. (Years of living with an alcoholic lets you know what "sober" is.)

At the end of the service, I walked back to him

because he wasn't able to come to me. He was crying. My father told me he had joined an alcoholic recovery program and been sober for three months as a graduation present to me.

The words "My prayer was answered" don't begin to convey the feelings I had at this time. God touched my father at a time when I finally let go of criticism and despair. Through a kind and sympathetic teacher, God brought us together: my music teacher had called him to see if he could attend this wedding to hear me play.

My father lived four years after that and then died of damage to his liver caused by excessive alcohol. During those four years we were able to travel and enjoy each other's company as father and daughter. The lost years became just that—lost years—and we were able to live in the present with the knowledge that God has a plan for each of us.

What is impossible with men is possible with God.
(Luke 18:27, RSV)

 Marie Asner is a church musician, poet, writer, entertainment reviewer and workshop presenter in the Kansas City area. She has been invited to conduct a workshop at the 1998 American Guild of Organists convention, has been nominated for several prestigious poetry awards and has had over fifty articles published plus numerous radio and TV appearances. Contact her at P.O. Box 4343 Overland Park, Kansas 66204-0343. Fax her at 1-913-385-5369.

The Woman Who Wouldn't Be Loved

Caron Loveless

I can hear my parents talking with the doctor in the living room, and I know something is wrong. Even though I'm thirteen, no one will tell me what's going on. It's not their policy to inform children about anything, even if it concerns their very near future. I know my father is sick. What I don't know is how soon he will die and leave me and my two younger sisters alone with a hard, angry stepmother.

For ten months I watch my thirty-four-year-old father slowly die of cancer. But before he dies he makes arrangements for our stepmother to adopt us. At the courthouse I want to tell the judge what my stepmother is really like. When he asks me, "Do you want to live with your stepmother and be adopted by her?" I sit silent for a half second.

This pause is the only power I have. My stepmom holds her breath. Why does she want us when she doesn't love us? Knowing I don't have a choice, I say, "Yes, I guess so."

My father dies. And within the year my step-mother brings home a new husband.

Mom doesn't go to church, but she thinks it's good for me. I don't complain because church is a haven. The people there care about me. They teach me to sing, to study the Bible; they encourage me to pray for my stepmother. I hear testimonies from addicts, athletes and alcoholics about how lost they were when God found them. They say if Christ could save them, He could save anyone. Then I go home and get punished for being late. I'm sure Christ can save me and those addicts, athletes and alcoholics. But my stepmom is as far from salvation as anyone on earth.

One day, I visit my stepmother's office while she's out. Her coworker says she's heard all about me and that my stepmom is very proud of me. How strange. I wonder why she lied to the people at work. At home she never says, "You look pretty today." She doesn't hug me. She never plays Scrabble or brushes my hair. She never asks, "What's your favorite color?" or "Do you need help with your homework?" But she does say, "You all are driving me to the nuthouse."

No matter how hard I try to please her, I'm always in trouble. I say, "Yes, ma'am" and "No ma'am" and never wrinkle my bedspread or talk back. Still, she yells and looks angry which makes me think she's ready to hit me. Her punishments never fit the crime. When I'm sixteen, she grounds me for the entire summer when I forget to feed the dog.

It's hard being a Christian at my house. When I make a mistake, my stepmother says, "And I thought you were supposed to be a Christian."

Each week I trim the grass that grows next to the fence with hand clippers. Mom likes the yard perfect. Thoughts boil up inside me. I hate her severe penalties, her ranting and raving. I hate her even though I know I'm not supposed to hate.

Then, from somewhere else comes a thought that can't be mine. It's such a compassionate thought that it must be from God: *Your stepmother can't help the way she is. What she does reflects her own neglected childhood. She's doing the best she can. Forgive her.*

It's like a revelation. For the first time, I see my stepmother's pain through the eyes of Jesus.

Months later I walk in the house to find my stepmother beating my sister. She's been drinking again. She's been drinking every day since her divorce. My sister was hiding the car keys so that mom couldn't go to the liquor store. Because no one tells my stepmother she can't do something, she goes out of control, slapping and pushing my sister to the floor.

I grab her arms and yell, "Stop hitting her right now! Get out of here and go to your room!" I'm shocked when she whimpers like a child and obeys me.

The summer I get married Mom disappears. For several months she leaves me to take care of my sisters, completely plan and pay for the wedding. As she walks out the door she tells me, "The psychiatrist says you girls are my problem, so I have to get away." This sounds fishy to me, because, even though we're not perfect, we never get in trouble and always do what she says. I weep for my sisters who have to live with an aunt now that I'm gone.

After our honeymoon, I pick up the phone and hear Mom in a tirade. She's discovered the visit we made to a lawyer trying to help her. With cursing, she threatens, "If I ever see you again, I'll kill you!"

I'm petrified. I've experienced her wrath and I know what she's capable of. Then she severs all contact with me and my sisters. We are fatherless, homeless and now motherless. At church, when we pray for the lost, I lift up a weary request to God. "Lord, You are the only one who can help Mom. Please send someone, anyone, to touch her life."

While my husband, David, is in seminary, our first son is born. I ask David to locate my stepmother and tell her the news. Surely she would want to know if someone is born or dies. He finds her and, to my amazement, she asks him to bring the baby to see her the next time we're in town.

I'm not prepared for what takes place the day we carry the baby up the steps to my stepmother's apartment. "She's had a nervous breakdown; that's why she shakes," a caregiver informs us. With tears streaming down her face, my stepmother reaches out to hold her first grandchild. She repeats over and over again, "I'm so sorry, I'm so sorry."

She has never, ever said this. My sisters are there, crying too. I allow myself to feel a measure of hope for our shattered family.

Then God gives David and me a plan. We are to carry it out whether we get positive responses or not. His challenge is the ancient commandment we know so well, Deuteronomy 5:16, which says, "Honor your father and your mother, as the LORD your God has commanded you, so that you may live long and that it may go well with you." We are to base our honor on her position, not her performance.

At first, my stepmother is not used to this positive attention and refuses our attempts. She makes excuses for not seeing us. She has recurring bouts with alcohol. Some days it's sheer work to honor her, but then God reminds me of His lifelong patience with me.

We hug her every chance we get and tease her if she resists our affection. We tell her we love her every time we see her. I try to act normal the first time I hear her sheepish reply, "I love you too."

We find other ways to honor her. David helps her with finances, prepares her taxes, gives her insurance and retirement advice. He arranges for car maintenance. We often emphasize our intention to take care of her should anything happen to her. We also seat her at the head of the table for meals and create elaborate celebrations on her birthday and Mother's Day.

Eventually she feels comfortable enough to attend church with us. She laughs when my husband, a pastor, tells stories about her in his messages. Then, one Easter Sunday morning, I witness what I never thought possible. This same woman who once threatened to take my life at long last gives hers to Jesus Christ. I want to celebrate. It feels like a dream. She will now join me in heaven.

These days, walking back toward the nursery after church I am still amazed by what I see. Mom is standing there with a child in her arms.

She winks when her first grandchild walks up and gives her a squeeze—he's nineteen now. The families of my sisters hover nearby. Mom has spent the morning rocking, diapering and playing with little children.

My prayer for Mom was answered, and miraculously, the one God sent to touch her life was—me.

Love your enemies, bless them that curse you, do good to them that hate you, and pray for them which despitefully use you, and persecute you. (Matthew 5:44, KJV)

Caron Loveless serves alongside her husband, David, senior pastor of Discovery Church, Orlando, Florida, as worship leader and Director of Creative Communications. She is also a freelance writer and speaks at women's meetings, retreats and conferences in the U.S. and Canada. E-mail: CaronLove@aol.com

In Search of a Father

Chris Bennett

I remember the scene as if it happened only yesterday, though I was just four years old at the time. My parents were sitting in the kitchen across the table from one another. My father stared blankly out the window with that stern Ottawa Indian bearing of his, a picture I have carried in my memory for so many years. My mother was in tears. I could tell he didn't want to look at her. Her pain was obvious. His pain was there too, I'm sure, but it wasn't as easy to see. Shortly after that, my parents divorced.

As I recall, it was harder on my brother than it was on me. He was older and had a better understanding of what was happening than I did. At my young age, I thought the divorce meant only that my father was going to move to an apartment building two blocks away, and that I could walk down there every day and take his mail to him. I

didn't know it meant he would be leaving us—
leaving our lives—permanently.

After my parents divorced, I seldom saw my father. As the years passed, our contacts became
even more infrequent. Finally I realized that if I
wanted to see him, it was up to me—I would have
to initiate the contact.

I kept reaching out to him, only to be rejected
time and again. On my sixteenth birthday, for example, my father had promised to visit me, but
never showed up. To say I was disappointed
would be a gross understatement. It didn't matter
that I had a great mother, a wonderful stepfather
and lots of friends. What I wanted most was the
love and approval of my father.

I finally got to a point when I thought to myself: *It's evident that my brother and I don't matter to
our father. I'm tired of it, tired of getting nothing but
rejection from him.* And so I gave up. For many
years neither my older brother nor I had any contact with our father—none whatsoever.

Fast-forward now to several years later. I had
matured and gone through college and seminary. I
was now a pastor and very much committed to the
principles and teachings I had learned about in my
involvement with Promise Keepers.

One of the seven promises of Promise Keepers
stresses the concept of reconciliation. Often this
refers to reconciliation between spouses, between
races or between denominations. But deep inside,
I knew that there was a wall between my father
and me that needed to be torn down. Things were

going well in my ministry, yet I felt I had a spiritual stumbling block. I knew there was a part of my life that was just "not right."

I thought about the many times I had heard people, particularly young men, tell about how their fathers had died before they had an opportunity to set things right with them or tell them they loved them. I knew one young man who actually ended up in a hospital because of the grief he felt over losing his father without having resolved things prior to his father's death. I even preached about this situation in my sermons. And yet, there I was in the same situation. I recognized the problem, but fear of further rejection kept me from doing anything about it.

I prayed for a resolution. Finally, about two-and-a-half years ago, it came. My wife, Marisa, our two daughters and I were on vacation in northern Michigan. I knew my father had retired to a reservation in that area. He is a member of the Grand Traverse Band of Ottawa and Chippewa Indians. While my wife and daughters were doing some shopping in Sutton's Bay, I went to the public library and looked through the area phone books until I found a listing for my father. I got directions and discovered we were not far from where he lived.

When Marisa and the girls returned to the car, I suggested we go for a drive. After a few minutes, we came to the location I was seeking. I drove down a long, sloping driveway and pulled up in front of a house.

"Well, who lives here?" Marisa asked.

"My father does," I answered.

She sat in stunned silence while I went up and knocked on the door. He wasn't home. I tried the tribal headquarters, across the street, but still didn't find him. I was directed to a third building.

There I entered an empty hallway where I saw a man walking toward me. As he approached I recognized him—*it was my father, walking right toward me!* It was an overpowering feeling.

I spoke his name. He looked at me with no sign of recognition.

"Do you know who I am?" I asked.

"No," he said.

"I'm your son, Chris," I told him. Impulsively and spontaneously, I reached out to hug him.

At first he was stiff, seemingly in shock. But then he relaxed, and we embraced and talked. We went outside where he met my family and invited us to meet his wife and go out for dinner. After dinner that night, we all went for a walk along a pier by Lake Michigan. As we walked, Marisa and my daughters were walking ahead with my step-mother while my dad and I lagged behind.

At first, our conversation was light and impersonal. Then suddenly, my father turned, looked at me intently and stated: "We *must* stay in touch!"

A few days later, at my father's invitation, we attended a Native American celebration. My father holds the position of Tribal Chairman in our tribe. He is also influential in Native American affairs with the U.S. government. He walked around the meeting with me, introducing me to important dignitaries—as his son! I could tell he was proud.

Since that time, a real closeness has developed between us. His religious foundations are different from mine, but he came to California a few months ago and heard me preach for the first time. It was a special time for both of us. I introduced him to my parishioners and friends—as my father! I think he could tell how proud I was.

One of the highlights of my father's visit was when we went to one of Southern California's world-famous amusement parks together. We never had an opportunity to go to one when I was young. Though I am now forty-one years old, you're never too old to go to an amusement park with your father. It was a very happy moment for me.

In Malachi 4:5-6 we read: "See, I will send you the prophet Elijah before that great and dreadful day of the LORD comes. He will turn the hearts of the fathers to their children, and the hearts of the children to their fathers. . . ." That passage has great personal importance to me, although I can honestly say now that I believe that my father, deep down, always did love us—his children—even through all those painful years. For a long time he didn't know how to show it, but now he is able to do that. He has grown and so have I.

I frequently talk with my father on the phone. He asks about my church and the people there. He has a great respect for the work I am doing in my ministry. I have a great respect for him and his work with our tribe. We have torn down the walls of bitterness and misunderstanding that stood between us for so many years. In place of those walls, we have *turned our hearts toward each other*, forming cords of reconciliation and love.

 Chris Bennett is Senior Pastor of the First Baptist Church of Laguna Hills, California. He and his wife, Marisa, have been married nineteen years and are the parents of two teenage daughters, Mackenzie and Carling. Recently transplanted from Michigan to California, his passion, apart from family and ministry, is surfing.

Never Give Up

Carole Neidhardt

"If you ever bring up religion in this house again, you can never go back to church," my parents declared when I told them I had received Christ as my Savior and that they could too.

I was only twelve years old, but I knew this new life journey I had begun as a born-again Christian was one that could enrich the lives of my family as well. It was not only dismissed as "an emotional experience I would soon outgrow," but it was something they refused even to consider as a possibility for themselves.

I was not prepared for their rejection, but didn't want to jeopardize my new life now that it had a meaning and purpose. I committed my parents' lives to Christ, faithfully prayed for their salvation and made a vow *never to give up*.

I did not speak of religion in our home. But I became active in my church youth group. My youth pastor was a real encouragement, as were many of the adult volunteers that ran the church youth programs.

Occasionally I could get my parents to come to church at Christmas or Easter. But essentially the church was my moral compass and separate from my home life. I would come home from a Youth For Christ meeting on Saturday nights, stop by the kitchen to say good night to my parents and find them playing poker, drinking and smoking.

When I graduated from high school, my church gave me a scholarship to Biola University. I was determined to go and get my "MRS" degree, thereby assuring me of the Christian family I so desperately sought. But I did not meet the "right" man that year. I left Biola for a less expensive community college feeling angry at God. I knew it was His will that I have a Christian family. What in the world was taking Him so long?!

I confess I did not handle this disappointment well. I stopped attending church and spent more time with my parents and non-Christian friends. I turned away from God, but fortunately He did not turn away from me. Each time I dated a man I thought I might have a future with, I prayed to God that He would send him away if he was not "Mr. Right."

When I finally met Dave, I considered not praying the "Get rid of him if he's not the right one" prayer. After all, I was getting a lot of pressure from my family to get married. At the ripe old age of twenty-four, I wasn't getting any younger! But I did pray that prayer, and God

didn't get rid of him. So, of course, I did marry
Dave, following an eighteen-month courtship.

After five years of marriage and two beautiful
children, I had a family but I still did not have a
Christian family. I realized I hadn't followed the
apostle Paul's admonition in Second Corinthians
6:14 about not being "yoked together with unbe-
lievers." But I also remembered the passage in
First Peter 3:1-2, where that apostle tells how unbelieving husbands "may be won over without
words by the behavior of their wives, when they
see the purity and reverence of your lives."

I began attending a local evangelical church. My
husband attended with me occasionally. I took my
kids to Sunday school every Sunday and became
an active member.

Through the ministry of our pastor, some dear
saints in that church and myself, my husband
came to a saving knowledge of Jesus Christ, as did
my children. I rejoiced that, at last, I had my
Christian family.

But God wasn't finished yet.

My husband challenged me to pick the most
"difficult" member of my family and we would
pray them to Christ. Within a couple of years, as a
direct result of our witness, my grandmother received Christ. She was not comfortable sharing
her decision with the rest of the family, but wrote
us a letter telling us all about her newfound faith
in Christ and the neighborhood Bible study she
was attending.

Several months later, Grandma died. We read

her letter to our family and shared our joy with them that she was rejoicing in heaven with Jesus.

Soon after that, both my parents, as well as my aunt and uncle, surrendered their lives to Christ. After twenty-seven years, the family I had prayed faithfully for had come to a saving knowledge of Jesus Christ. I never gave up, but more importantly, *He* never gave up.

God is faithful in all His promises. We who believe in Christ know this, but we get caught up in our own time line, and we sometimes forget that He accomplishes *His* perfect will in *His* perfect time—not ours.

If you have loved ones that you have been praying for, don't give up. God hears your prayers. He will accomplish His will in His time. Be faithful. Believe even when all seems impossible. With God, all things are possible. Our God is an awesome God. He never gives up.

I will sing of the LORD's great love forever; with my mouth I will make your faithfulness known through all generations. (Psalm 89:1)

Carol Neidhardt is a native Californian who has resided in Dana Point for the past thirty years. She and her husband, David, have two grown children, Sharilyn and David, III. Carol works at a major newspaper and writes in her spare time. She and her husband are active members at San Clemente Presbyterian Church.

Second-Chance Parenting

Karen O'Connor

I married a man I was crazy about from the day I met him. But before our tenth anniversary it was clear we did not share the same values or dreams. I began feeling alone in the marriage. He was consumed by his law practice and I was consumed by our home and children. For years I had been too busy to notice the imbalance. But as the children got older and needed less of my time, I had more opportunity to see the void in my life.

By the time we were married just under twenty years, my husband met someone he preferred over me. Shortly afterward he moved out of our home. In the weeks that followed, I cried, screamed, drove for hours and sobbed myself to sleep. Then one day, I vowed that I would keep the kids and me together no matter what.

But my resolve lasted only two weeks. Suddenly, unexpectedly, I fell apart completely. My health went. My emotions broke. I was a wreck. I realized that I had been running on empty for a long time. I couldn't think, feel, decide, choose or plan. Grief flooded over me like a tidal wave. There were days when I thought I would drown in sorrow.

Over the next year and a half, my husband and I went back and forth, but we couldn't stay together. His heart was with the other woman. We separated, divided up our possessions and filed for divorce.

My son and youngest daughter remained in the family home with their father, and our oldest daughter and I moved to an apartment nearby until she left for college.

As my children moved into adulthood, their deeper pain flared up. My youngest daughter expressed her grief through rebellion as a teenager. My son buried himself in sports and smoking pot. And my oldest daughter dealt with her pain by escaping overseas as a student, then as a missionary.

I handled mine by moving to another city, away from the scene of past hurts, and eventually remarrying.

Visits with my son and youngest daughter were both precious and painful. I hated to see them end. I felt like the weekend parent who spoils them with movies and toys, but who misses out on the day-to-day events that will never pass this way again.

I coped by jumping on the merry-go-round of self-improvement seminars and workshops and New Thought "churches" that were so prevalent during the 1980s. None of them had the answers I longed for. So I turned to the Bible and read God's Word for myself instead of relying on the metaphysical interpretation I had been taught.

This experience transformed my mind—and heart. The truth about Jesus as my Lord and Savior came home to me. In December of 1982, I had the most beautiful experience of my life one morning on the beach as I returned from my morning walk. I stopped to pray, and in those few moments I felt, in a deep way, the Lord comforting me and assuring me that He was real and could be trusted; that He could be known in a personal way—a way that could make a difference in my life.

Four years later my youngest daughter came to live with my second husband and me while attending junior college. During that time our relationship took an important turn. I had experienced emotional and spiritual healing by then, so I knew that, finally, I had something to give her.

There were times of turbulence as she experienced bouts of depression and grief. There were also long walks along the ocean together, hours of talking and crying, and times of angry confrontation when she told me how she felt about the divorce, her feelings of being abandoned by me and her fear of being alone. And it was a time of deep inner healing as she began building a relationship with Christ. We attended church together regularly.

Meanwhile, my oldest daughter was living overseas. Our relationship had always been good. She
had been my closest confidant following my divorce. I realize now, however, that I leaned on her
too heavily.

A few years ago, shortly after she and her family
moved back to the United States from Morocco, her
pain broke loose. The reality of what she had come
home to was there in front of her. Her father lived
in one city; I lived in another. There was no conti-
nuity from the past to carry her through the transi-
tion to her new life in the United States.

She let out her emotions in spurts at first. She
took swipes at me, answered abruptly and seemed
angry whenever we were together. Then one Saturday it all came out—in a torrent of accusations,
fear, anger, hostility and deep hurts. For the first
time in my life with her, I felt like the enemy. She
seemed to hate me—for who I was, for what I had
done, for what I had not done. I was a major disappointment and she let me know it.

Months passed and we exchanged letters and
cards, attempting to let one another know how we
felt. It was one of the most painful experiences of
my life. I grieved the loss of the daughter I had
loved and been close to for nearly thirty years.

I didn't realize at the time we were on the brink
of a new birth in our relationship. And we each
needed time to look at one another afresh in the
light of our individual maturing process. We both
realized that we hadn't been completely honest
with one another.

I also had a problem expressing anger toward her—toward anyone for that matter. It took time—months of letter writing, periods of silence and tentative communications as we shared little by little—and then a breakthrough came when the Lord spoke privately to each one of us about the other.

She came to an understanding of my pain and I came to an understanding of hers. Expressing these insights to one another accelerated the healing process and opened us up in a new way to feeling the love that was there all along.

I learned to listen to her feelings instead of fixing them, how to share without burdening her, how to remain her parent and become her friend, how to acknowledge her point of view without feeling threatened.

Today, our relationship is real—not perfect. I can now relate to her as a whole person, rather than as a fearful, grief-stricken, guilt-ridden parent.

As for my son, we've always been able to talk and share honestly. He has been able to express some of his feelings toward me. He has raged at me, cried with me, shared the intense pain he feels in his relationship with his father. I treasure these moments, tough as they are to live through. They show me that his heart has not hardened. He knows that I love him. I know that he loves me and has forgiven me.

The consequences of my choices—to leave the family home, to remarry, to become a Christian—

are there as we go forward. But we are moving into a new level of healed emotions, understanding and, most important to me, a deep and abiding friendship.

Today my son and daughters are in their thirties. It took nearly a decade to face and deal with our past. For a long time it was easy to focus our blame on their father. But a divorce is never clean-cut. No one person is ever completely at fault.

Grief can be lifted and guilt can be dismissed when we accept God's cleansing. He knows the truth about me, about my children, about my situation—and yours. He can comfort us so we can bounce back from grief or from anything that seems to separate us from His love.

God has shown me through this experience the truth of First John 1:9: "If we confess our sins, he is faithful and just and will forgive us our sins and purify us from all unrighteousness."

Karen O'Connor is an award-winning author/speaker, known for her inspiring books and presentations on topics from "women and money" to "intimacy in relationships." She is also a writing consultant and a seminar leader for churches, schools and professional organizations. She and her husband live in San Diego, California. E-mail: WordyKaren@aol.com

Chapter 5

Growing through Grief

He heals the brokenhearted and binds up their wounds. (Psalm 147:3)

Times of Joy and Sorrow

Fred Littauer

By 1960, Florence and I had two healthy and beautiful little girls, Lauren and Marita, ages five and one. I loved my two daughters and did everything I knew to do to be the best father I could be for them. However, like many fathers, I also wanted to have a son.

In 1961 our first son was born. I gave him my name, fulfilling my ambition to sire Frederick J. Littauer, III. He too was a bright and beautiful child. But when little Freddie was about six months old, he began to wake up screaming during the night. Florence took him to our pediatrician, expecting the doctor to diagnose a minor illness. Instead, he told Florence bluntly, "This child is hopelessly brain damaged."

A specialist gave us the same, heartbreaking diagnosis. All our willpower, all the money in the world, could not help my little namesake.

The doctors recommended we put him in a private children's nursing home in Northern Connecticut where he would receive the loving attention and care he needed. We did as they suggested.

After Freddie was diagnosed, the doctors said there was no explanation for the brain deterioration and they advised us to have another child. It was not long before our second son was born, and we chose a name related to Florence's family: Laurence Chapman Littauer.

Little Larry was carefully tested at birth to make certain he was completely healthy. The report was 100 percent positive. We rejoiced, even though our Freddie was still in that children's home, now blind, deaf and without any human faculties.

Little Larry developed normally, and we became a family in recovery. Six months after Larry's birth, we received a call from the nursing home telling us Freddy, now two years old, had strangled and died in the night. We had many emotions to deal with, including grief and loss. We struggled with the question some friends and relatives had raised: "Should we have kept him home with us?"

One week later Florence went into little Larry's room and, as she frequently did, waved her hand across his face. No response. She tapped her hand on the crib rail. He was awake, but there was no response. She picked him up and cried, "Smile, Larry, smile!" But Larry didn't smile.

Emotions poured over her as she recognized the same lack of reactions she had seen in Freddie. Quickly she took him to the same doctor who had examined Freddie. She says she will never forget the look on the doctor's face. After a brief examination he told her quietly, "Florence, I'm sure it's the same thing."

Both Florence and I were in shock. How could this happen a second time? Our two daughters were normal and healthy. Why not our two sons? What was wrong? Once again there were no answers. This time, however, we took Larry to Johns Hopkins Hospital in Baltimore to have a brain biopsy. Again the answer came back: "There is no hope." Larry did not have a normal brain. The doctors told us he would never live beyond five years of age.

I brought him home on the plane, his little head swathed in bandages. From that day on he was no more than a living vegetable. He could not hear or see and soon had no responses whatsoever. Once again, we had to make a decision. I will never forget the day we bundled little Larry up and drove him to Northern Connecticut to that same children's home where his brother had died just a few months before.

I continued to visit him periodically, even after we moved to California in 1968. I will never forget one of those visits. I had flown to Connecticut from California on a business trip. I decided to make the two-hour drive through the Connecticut countryside to visit my son.

When I entered this large converted home, I turned to the room on the right. There were many cribs in that room, and on the door frame was a list of the names of the little children there, all pitiful examples of something gone awry.

I looked in vain on the list for my son's name. I walked to the big room on the left side of the house. Larry's name was not on that list either. But inside the room I saw an attendant feeding a child about the size of a seven-year-old. The girl's body looked normal but her head was a fraction of normal size. I walked over to this kindly woman, wondering how anyone could work in a place such as this, probably with very low pay and rarely any thanks.

In a halting voice I said, "Excuse me, but I'm looking for my son. His name is Larry Littauer."

"Oh yes," was her gentle reply, "I know where he is. Please come with me." She led me to the second floor. We passed through a room with three or four cribs and into an adjoining room. There she pointed to a little child lying on a cushion on the floor.

Then she left the room so I could visit with my son, the child on the cushion. Visit with him! How does one *visit* with someone who is blind and deaf and doesn't even know you are there! I had driven two hours to see my little son and I couldn't "visit" with him. He was now about sixteen years old, but still the same size he was when we took him there—when he was one. All I could do was to stand over him and weep and pray.

As I continued to stand over him and to talk to my heavenly Father about my son, I prayed, "Lord, take him home, for his life is so wasted."

Instantly I heard a response, a message I have never forgotten. It was the first time I had heard this voice speak to me. Clearly in my head I heard, "His life is no more wasted than is your life when you're not serving Me, no more wasted than the life of any Christian who just sits in church on Sunday morning."

Without question I knew who had spoken to me. As I drove away from the nursing home, those words kept ringing in my mind. Now I knew why I had been led to drive that long distance to visit a son who would not even know I was there. My Father in heaven had a message He wanted me to hear. He needed me to be there. He wanted me to cry out to Him.

Suddenly, instead of feeling depressed and discouraged, I had a joy and exuberance in my soul. Over and over again God's words came to me: *His life is no more wasted than is your life when you're not serving Me, no more wasted than the life of any Christian who just sits in church on Sunday morning.*

The doctors had told us Larry would not live longer than about five years. Larry died when he was nineteen years old, still the same size he had been when we had taken him to the nursing home when he was one.

As a dear Christian friend once pointed out to

us, both Freddie and Larry gave their lives that we might find life. This is true because it was during that memorable visit to see Larry that I first heard God's voice speaking directly to me. And it was in 1965, after Freddie had died, that Florence had reluctantly agreed to go to a Christian Women's Club meeting. There she heard—*really heard*—the gospel for the first time.

Agreeing that she needed help, she asked the Lord Jesus to give her a new life. Several months later, in God's sovereign timing, a pastor came to our door and invited Florence to come to his church. She took the girls and went the very next day.

On the following Sunday, at the urging of my two daughters, I went to church as well. As a family we quickly became faithful regulars. After attending this church consistently for twelve months, I responded to the call of the Savior. As I sat there in the service that Sunday I heard the pastor say four times to others in the congregation, "I see your hand."

He waited and then asked again, "Anyone else?" I could wait no longer. I knew that I too needed a change in my life. If Jesus offered hope, this was where I needed to be.

I raised my hand.

Editor's note: Fred and Florence adopted a son after the loss of their first two sons. They named him Freddie. See Florence Littauer's story in Chapter 1.

God is our refuge and strength, an ever-present help in trouble. (Psalm 46:1)

Fred Littauer is a graduate of New York University and has been in business for himself for most of his life. In 1984 Fred turned his focus to full-time speaking, writing and managing his wife Florence's speaking schedule and office. He has written seven books, including three that he coauthored with Florence. They reside in Palm Springs, California.

The Vacuum

Suzy Ryan

The vacuum cleaner broke, and my heart felt broken too. *Why am I so upset just because my sweeper is on the blink?* I wondered.

My brother, Bart, sold me the vacuum six months before he killed himself. As a newlywed I didn't have the money for the expensive vacuum, but knowing that no one else in the family would buy one from him, I did.

Why did I feel such responsibility for my brother? I was all Bart had, or at least that's how I felt. My two siblings and I all had different fathers. My younger brother needed me, and I needed him to need me.

Sadly, Bart's disorder was deeper than I knew. He suffered with manic depression, something I didn't comprehend. His charming personality and chiseled good looks made him appear like a healthy young man. Though bright and witty, he never had any friends, never made good grades, never experienced success. Although he pretended to prefer remaining home alone, I saw his dejected blue eyes, desperate for acceptance. His insecurity and solitary life broke my heart!

Determined to compensate for his suffering, I allowed him to live in my shadow. Bart attended football games to watch me cheerlead. He kept the gold medals I'd earned from running track. As I lifeguarded at the town pool, Bart sat beside my chair. He trailed me, and I loved it! He filled a void that all my achievements could not fill.

When I left for college I felt as if I'd abandoned my own son. As I was driving away I glanced guiltily in my rearview mirror. Bart was pedaling his bike as fast as he could, yelling out, "Please hurry home, Suz. I'm going to miss you!" It took everything I had not to turn around and take my eleven-year-old brother with me.

When our mother married again, she took Bart and left the state, so I didn't see him during his high school years. It wasn't until I got married that our relationship resumed. He was seventeen, and though he had attempted suicide in tenth grade, I thought he was now on the road to becoming a healthy-minded adult.

He got a job selling vacuums and spent the weekends with my husband and me at our condo. We enjoyed the beach, restaurants, tennis and just reminiscing together.

One unexpected visit concerned me. His car broke down and Bart called me, needing a place to stay. Something was different about him. Mom had told me she thought he was into drugs. Concerned, I sat Bart down and said, "I love you and I am here for you. Mom told me you might be into cocaine, and I'm worried."

"Oh, Suz," he replied, "you know Mom exaggerates. She can't tell me what to do now that I'm on my own, and she doesn't like that. I'm fine."

I couldn't deny that our mother, like many mothers, loved to control her children, so I believed him. Still, when he drove off the next day, I had a fleeting, painful thought: *I'll never see him again.*

How could I know this prophetic feeling was accurate? Bart disappeared. Through those two silent days I prayed, "God, make him call!"

Bart never called. Instead, two days after he disappeared his body was found in the car, along with drugs. He had taken his life by carbon monoxide poisoning.

I knew I needed to take hold of God's strength in this tragedy. But how? In the following weeks I obediently trudged to church, but I was numb. I hoped maybe I would hear a song that would console me. I taught Sunday school, and sometimes, through my numbness, I would hear a Scripture verse.

My husband and friends were encouraging but impatient, wondering, "What's happened to the 'old Suzy'?"

Working hard at my sales job provided relief during the day, but nighttime became my enemy when all sleeping ceased. For the first time in my highly organized life, I was immobilized. Sleep deprivation and exhaustion left me treading waters of despair.

My aunt suggested I attend her nondenominational group called Bible Study Fellowship. In studying the Word, I experienced God's love. I learned to apply Scripture to my life situations. Surrendering my memories to God, I allowed the tears to flow freely. Meditating on God's promises seemed like balm to my broken heart.

As those promises salved the raw, deep gash left in my spirit by the loss of my brother, I began sleeping again. Depression disappeared as God's love pulled me from the pool of despair.

I thought I had finally recovered from Bart's death. That is, until the day my vacuum broke, and I couldn't bear to throw it away. I deluded myself into thinking that the vacuum was a link to our cherished memories, which I desperately wanted to keep alive. I had never forgiven myself for letting him leave that dreadful day.

Questions burned in my heart. Silently I wondered: *Could I have prevented him from committing suicide? By leaving for college, did I forsake him? Should I have found a psychiatrist and insisted on therapy for Bart?*

And what about Mom? I couldn't blame her for Bart's choice. I too experienced our mom's lifestyle, but I didn't kill myself. Actually, I feel sorry for my mom. I know what grief I experienced losing my brother. I'm sure her feelings of guilt must be overwhelming!

I know I'll never understand Bart's life or why he felt the need to end it. But, in thinking about the vacuum cleaner, I realized that just as time broke my vacuum, life broke Bart. I don't have any idea why Bart killed himself. When I get to heaven, I know that I'll receive the answers.

Tomorrow I go vacuum shopping. My children will be with me. Ten years have passed and I am finally ready to part with the sweeper that kept Bart's memory vividly alive. As I throw away the worn appliance, I'm ready to let go of my sense of accountability for my brother and concentrate instead on God's gifts.

Bart will always hold a tender place in my heart, but the vacuum in my life caused by his death is now being filled by the peace of Christ and my three precious children. God truly is restoring the years the locusts had eaten.

I will repay you for the years the locusts have eaten. (Joel 2:25)

Suzy Ryan lives in Southern California with her husband and three small children. Her articles have appeared in *Today's Christian Woman*, *Woman's World*, *The American Enterprise* and various newspapers. E-mail her at KenSuzyR@aol.com

For They Shall Be Comforted

Gwen Bagne

As I pulled up near the grave, a car was parked across the cemetery. The woman inside waved. We met that afternoon at her husband's grave. Stepping out of our automobiles, we walked toward each other. Although we'd only spoken on the phone and never met face-to-face, when we reached each other, we embraced like old friends. "I'm Gwen," I said.

She responded, "I'm Sandy."

Sandy spread a small blanket beside her husband's grave. As we sat down, it all seemed so natural. Slowly and tenderly, she began to pull memories of her husband out of the basket she held in her hands. Sandy showed me pictures of her wedding, the children and the funeral. She was only six months into her widowhood. Her eyes filled with tears as she opened her broken heart to me.

I listened quietly to the familiar story, similar to the stories I have heard many times in the last three years. She told me all the details of the last day of Martin's life. She described to me that morning, as Martin kissed her good-bye, and then one hour later, as a police officer came to her door telling her there had been an automobile accident. She told how her life stopped that day and has never been the same.

I am always touched by the stories I hear and feel honored that God has given me the opportunity to share in the journeys to recovery which lie ahead.

I began my own journey through grief with no real understanding of what was ahead of me. I could only see what I had lost. Three years earlier, I had stood in front of the casket that held the love of my life, my husband Steve. I asked God, "How do I leave this viewing room and go on living?"

I had been a single mom with two little boys and had been a Christian for two years when I was introduced to Steve Bagne in a Singles Bible study. Friends from the start, our friendship grew into love, and we married two years later.

God gave me exceedingly, abundantly more than I had ever asked for. We were married for twelve years; we had raised my children together; we were out of debt and teaching Bible principles to others. I will always remember that year as "the sweet year."

Then, after a routine examination, Steve was diagnosed with acute leukemia. We were devastated, but then experienced the miracle of finding a bone marrow donor. Steve went through a painful bone marrow transplant at the Cancer Research Center in Seattle. He came home four months later for the long process of recovery.

We knew the first year was critical, but felt confident we had come through the worst, because so many others did not even make it far enough to walk out of the hospital.

On a beautiful April morning, after he had been home for five months, he had a severe headache that took us back to where it had all begun. Many bone marrow patients are readmitted the first year, so we were not alarmed.

Three days later we were told it was a chicken pox infection, also common for transplant patients. This infection was in Steve's brain. Soon he was lying in a coma on life support systems.

Nine days after we came to check out a headache, the doctors told me to prepare myself. How could I possibly prepare myself for this? Six hours later, as I leaned over Steve, the doctor touched my shoulder and said, "It's over."

Over! The moment had come, when my friend, sweet husband and love, breathed his last. All the people gathered there began to weep. Steve was dead and I drove home a widow. Although the sun was still shining, my world went dark as if a curtain had dropped before my eyes.

A few days later, beside the casket, I not only

asked, "How do I leave the viewing room and go on living," but *"Why* should I go on living?"

God, always faithful to His Word, never leaves us comfortless. He sent a young widow named Marilyn into my life. She listened to me and gave me hope. When I was helpless and hopeless, she told me joy would come back into my life, that the sun would shine again. I believed her, because she had survived the same loss a few years earlier. She took my hand to help me cross the river of grief.

Now it's my turn. I take Sandy's hand and help her cross that river. We stood together in the graveyard, knowing the same grief and the same God. The truth of Second Corinthians 1:4 suddenly came alive for me: "[He] comforts us in all our troubles, so that we can comfort those in any trouble with the comfort we ourselves have received from God." As I drove home from the cemetery, I was acutely aware that our steps are ordained by God.

Jesus told Peter once that Satan wished to sift him. Jesus prayed for Peter that his faith would not fail and told him, "[Peter], when you have turned back, strengthen your brothers" (Luke 22:32). So it is with all of us who are sifted by life's circumstances. Once we are back on our feet, we are to strengthen someone else, to pass it on.

God helps us bounce back with new purpose and new strength in Him. He desires that we help others, and therefore, we do more than just survive—we thrive!

 Gwen Bagne presents seminars educating and motivating others to prepare in practical ways for untimely death, and giving hope and guidance to those left behind. She has written two booklets on these topics. She also speaks on other life issues. She lives in Milton, Washington and may be reached at (253)874-5082 or e-mail GBagne@aol.com

Chapter 6

Overcoming Financial Stress

Dear friend, I pray that you may enjoy good health and that all may go well with you, even as your soul is getting along well. (3 John 1:2)

True Financial Freedom

Paul J. Lauterjung

*D*o you long to have financial freedom in your life? What does this
freedom mean to you? To me it used
to mean having enough money to pursue my
dreams; it meant making more money in order to
support my "dream" lifestyle. But the events I will
share with you showed me what being financially
free is *really* all about.

My wife and I were professionals earning in the
top ten percent of families in this country. We
were working in corporate America, providing so-
lutions in business systems and finance. But our
spending habits were increasing as our income
grew. In pursuit of success and a better lifestyle,
we were losing control of our financial stability.
One day, we finally realized and admitted, *We
have no idea how to create financial stability in our own*

lives with the money we're earning. Although we were saving and owned a house, much of our money was slipping through our fingers. We were chasing after money and losing the race.

The final straw was when we decided to go into business for ourselves. We left the corporate rat race, like so many millions of Americans do, to go out on our own to that blessed freedom called "Small Business Owner."

We were soon to learn, however, what it truly means to be in financial bondage! The cash we had saved was quickly gone, much of it invested in our business. We were up against a wall. Not enough money, a son to raise, a mortgage to pay, a future to consider. Our wall of debt was higher than we could have possibly imagined it getting— so high, in fact, that we couldn't see over the top.

We were educated, intelligent people wondering why we got ourselves into this financial mess and how were we going to get out. We lost sleep, consumed with anxiety about money. We felt guilty, unable to pay all our bills no matter how hard we tried. There was tension in our marriage.

The ironic part of all this was that we were financial counselors! We helped others set financial goals, get out of debt and live within their means. And now we had become our own best (or worst) clients. I was ashamed I had allowed this to happen. I felt helpless. I had been "downsized" twice in two years out of my corporate jobs and now felt a great loss of identity. I felt I couldn't even provide for my family.

Finally, one New Year's Day, in desperation I got down on my knees and surrendered our situation over to the Lord. I can't believe I hadn't done that before. I had been trying "my way" until I realized it was not the "best way." I told God I had no idea how we would even be able to pay our mortgage that month. (We were truly out of money!) But I had enough faith to say, "Lord, I trust You for providing. I need Your help and guidance. Please forgive me for trying to 'fix' the situation on my own."

When I got up from our bedroom floor and went to get the morning newspaper, I found two large bags of groceries with a note attached that said: "God has great plans for you!" On the other side of the note was the verse from Jeremiah 29:11. " 'For I know the plans I have for you,' declares the LORD, 'plans to prosper you and not to harm you, plans to give you hope and a future.' "

I was stunned—and moved to tears. It became obvious to me that all this time I was trying to do the "providing" on my own. Now I would allow God to provide and trust for His blessings. And blessings He gave! Shortly after the "groceries" miracle, we started receiving anonymous checks and gift certificates in the mail. Then one Sunday in March of that year, we dedicated our business to the Lord at our church service. The next day we got a phone call from a nationwide newspaper asking to do an interview and feature article on our business!

At the same time the article came out, I was offered and accepted a full-time position with a well-known insurance company. In a short time, we went from "famine" to feast! We received a flood of calls as a result of the article, and many of these calls turned into clients. Our own financial struggles now helped us to "speak from experience"!

We began to give more church seminars and share our testimony. In April, because of taxes being due, our expenses came to $9,900—and our income was $10,200! We know this miracle happened as a result of praying and giving up control to God. We had truly learned how to add "faith" to our finances.

As a man, I used to put great pride in "conquering" the job market and providing for my family. However, through this experience I realized that God is the Great Provider and "will meet all [my] needs according to his glorious riches in Christ Jesus" (Philippians 4:19). I found that true financial freedom is not freedom *with* money, but freedom *from* money; that is, freedom from worry about financial matters.

I've found that contentment and an "attitude of gratitude" for all the blessings that already surround me give me the proper perspective for knowing how to handle my money. I also learned how to give back from my "firstfruits" to the Lord.

If you are searching for financial freedom and security, may this story help and inspire you. I pray you will "be rich in good deeds, and . . . be generous and willing to share. In this way they will lay up treasure for themselves as a firm foundation for the coming age, so that they may take hold of the life that is truly life" (1 Timothy 6:18-19).

Paul J. Lauterjung (B.S.M., Pepperdine University) and his wife, Patricia, have extensive experience as cash flow consultants. They speak on a variety of topics using humor, inspiration and sound financial advice. Clients have included Mt. Hermon Christian Conference Center, American Express, churches and schools. They reside in Petaluma, California. Phone/fax them at (707) 765-9500.

Money– No Small Change

Andy and Vivian Baniak

Surely you desire truth in the inner parts; you teach me wisdom in the inmost place. (Psalm 51:6)

When we say the word "money," what comes to your mind? Each of us would have a different response to that question. Everyone has what we call a "life message" about money. Such a message ingrains itself in our mind early in life and affects our life-long emotional responses concerning money. If that life message is false, if it has not been changed by truth from the Word of God, problems in the area of personal finances will crop up sooner or later. That's how it was for us.

Andy grew up as child number ten in a West Virginia coal-mining family of thirteen children.

When he was five, his father drowned in a work-related ferryboat accident, leaving Andy's mother pregnant with child number thirteen. His mother raised the family on a meager miner's pension, Social Security and welfare until the children were old enough to go to work and help out. The family grew vegetables in a garden, augmented by staples that were given to them by Welfare.

Andy describes his childhood memories: "We never had enough money to make ends meet. School lunch was usually an apple butter sandwich. At dinner, I had to fill my plate quickly if I wanted to have anything to eat at a table of fourteen people. I was sixteen before I owned a pair of pants that were not hand-me-downs from my older brothers. Our family was the last family in our small town to get indoor plumbing.

"I remember how embarrassed I felt when I had to make up excuses to put off the bill collectors that came to our door. I realized that my only hope of ever having a better life was to leave West Virginia and the poverty of my family. At seventeen I joined the army. I sent money home from my army paycheck every month to help support my mother and younger siblings."

You get the picture—Andy grew up in abject poverty. These life circumstances formed Andy's life message about money. Underlying every financial decision he made was the thought, *I'll never be poor again.*

While Andy was growing up in West Virginia, Vivian was growing up in Mt. Rainier, Maryland, just outside Washington, DC. Her family's financial situation was a notch above Andy's. They had their own TV—a luxury for their family in the early 1950s. The six members of her blended family lived in a 1,000-square-foot semidetached brick home. Her father had a blue-collar job that enabled him to work overtime to provide a few extras for his growing family.

Vivian might have grown up with a relatively stable view of money had it not been for an event involving money that distorted her thinking.

In the early '50s, Saturday afternoon movie matinees were the place to be. One Saturday when Vivian was nine years old, alone in a darkened theater, she was stealthily molested by a man sitting next to her. The man gave her two dollars and left. Feeling shame and guilt, she ran to the candy counter at the back of the theater and tried to spend the money on candy as fast as she could to get rid of it. She feared that if she took the money home, her parents would ask her where she had gotten it.

Says Vivian: "As a young adult, even though I held a well-paying position as a legal secretary, I was never able to save money. After Andy and I married, he was surprised to discover that I simply could *not* hold onto money. If he gave me $50, it was soon spent. If he gave me $100, $200 or $500, it would disappear on items we really didn't need. What he didn't realize was that my life message about money was 'Get rid of it!' You can imagine what it was like for Mr. *I'll never be poor again!'* to marry Miss *'I've got to get rid of the money!'* "

Shortly after becoming Christians in their mid-thirties, Vivian and Andy began to study the Bible and what it taught about money. They learned there are five times as many verses about money as there are about prayer. They began to tithe. Within a year of their beginning to tithe, Andy got a job with World Vision, a major Christian humanitarian organization.

Today Andy, in his position with World Vision, is responsible for tracking millions of dollars in support of that organization's humanitarian and evangelistic efforts in the name of Christ.

"I know this organization is helping families all over the world just like the one I grew up in, back in West Virginia," Andy says. "I also know that our Heavenly Father is 'he who gives you power to get wealth' (Deuteronomy 8:18, RSV) and that 'God will supply every need of [ours] according to his riches in glory in Christ Jesus' (Philippians 4:19, RSV)."

In Vivian's case, it was not until her early forties, after seeking godly counseling, that she was able to get to the root of her problem with handling money: suppressed anger over her childhood molestation.

"I had never made the connection between the way I handled money and the emotionally traumatic incident that happened when I was a child," she says. "I needed to get to the root of my anger, and so I asked the Lord to do 'open-heart surgery' on me. God is so faithful. Through a Christian support group, I learned the root of my anger and money problems. At that point, I was able to replace false guilt and shame with truth.

"As Christians, we sometimes forget that after being saved, we are to live by the 'grace and truth [that] came through Jesus Christ' (John 1:17). We now more fully understand His intention to restore and rebuild the broken places in our lives, both for our good and for His glory. He changed our thinking about money—and that was no small change."

Andy and Vivian Baniak are co-founders of Money Mentors in Tacoma, Washington, a personal financial workshop teaching biblical principles of finance, personalized financial planning and family communication about money. Vivian is a Precept Ministries leader, a graduate of CLASS and a speaker for women's meetings and home-school groups. Andy, a retired army officer, has served for seventeen years with World Vision and is currently Finance Manager for World Vision U.S. Programs. E-mail: MMVIVIANDY@integrityol.com

In God I Trust

Gisele Guilbert

While there were good reasons, it was mostly the fact that my eyes were more ambitious than my wallet that explained why, at thirty years of age, I was $48,000 in debt.

The debt should have been overwhelming to me, but I felt secure. I boasted that my security was in God; but sadly, it was in the knowledge that, although I'd been reduced to earning a mere $1,200 a month, I could still borrow on a line of credit to make my monthly payments. I didn't worry about what would happen when the credit line dwindled, because I assumed another plastic card would always arrive just in the nick of time.

A year earlier I had found myself in the midst of a failed business and an annulled marriage. Confronted with my own inability to make my life succeed, I had finally come to the sweet place of surrendering my life to God and to the salvation of His Son, Jesus.

Now, while most of the pieces in my life were broken, I thought I was secure in the knowledge that with God all things are possible. In fact, one morning in a brief but heartfelt prayer I told Him how truly grateful I was for all He had done for me. I loved Him, loved the little house I'd been renting for the last seven years, loved my parents, my dog and yes, I truly trusted Him with all that I had!

Somewhere in the recesses of my heart I heard a tiny question, "Trust Me? Do you really trust Me?"

"Oh, yes, Lord," I whispered, my head still bowed, "I really do!"

Another question came: "Then why, if you trust Me, do you run to your line of credit every month for the money to pay your bills?"

Instantly my head came up, my eyebrows raised in shock. I responded, "Surely you're joking, Lord. I need over $2,000 a month just to pay the minimums. Without that extra money my credit would be ruined! I'd never be able to realize my dream to buy a house."

I remember the picture that came to my mind. I saw myself standing on a road leading into a deep pool of mud. I knew I would have to walk through it. I couldn't tell if it would be over my head, but I could see Jesus standing next to me, offering me His hand, saying, "If you trust Me and I choose this road for you, it's for a good reason—but I'll go with you."

I knew that I could trust Him, and so I agreed,

"OK, Lord, no more credit cards. I'll trust You to provide."

During the next few months I wrote letters to all my creditors, explaining that while I was unable to make the minimum payments on my loans, I would send small, good faith payments each month and intended to pay off the balances.

I didn't receive much understanding from the bill collectors. I cringed, recalling the judgment I had passed on others in similar situations. Daily my coworkers would head out the door for power lunches while I'd take my sandwich and Bible to the park. Writing my tithe check became more important as I learned that with the measuring cup (and attitude) I used when I gave, so God would measure back His giving to me. (See Luke 6:38.)

I learned to be honest about my situation and found that very few judged me harshly. At one point, I was counting on a commission check from my last job to cover my rent. Sorting through a huge pile of mail, I was distressed not to see the check and immediately phoned my old boss, Jim, who owed it to me. He heard the concern in my voice, yet he was angry because I had left his company. He said he was leaving for vacation and wouldn't have time to write the check until he returned.

He mocked my faith, asking me if I realized yet that God wasn't going to help me. I half-listened to him as I opened the mail and noticed a letter from my church. I was confused, because it wasn't a letter—it was a check made payable to me. I saw a notation on the memo line and was struck speechless.

On the other end of the phone, Jim waited for me to respond to his question about God. I explained I was momentarily distracted by the unexplained appearance of a check from my church!

Jim's voice crackled with condescension. "A check from your church? Why would a church send you a check?"

"Well, I'm not exactly sure, but there's a notation that says 'love gift.'"

"Love gift?" He was almost subdued by the unfamiliar words. "What's a love gift?"

"I think it's when someone knows you need help, and they give it to you through the church so you won't know who it is." I paused, struck by the implications of such a gesture.

"I think it means someone loves you. Loves *me*." My voice quivered as tears streamed down my cheeks. I had never experienced anything like this. Jim muttered that he had to go and my check would be in the mail.

That night I shared the remarkable experience with my new roommate. We laughed over God's sense of humor and timing.

Over the next year many events showed me how God provides each step of the way. There was the time the IRS threatened to seize my checking account, and the same day a refund check arrived from my insurance carrier for an accident that had occurred over five years earlier.

One very special gift I received from Him was

the one I gave away. It was my first shopping trip to the mall in months. I had saved for a new suit and found one at half price, leaving me with almost $50 to spare. I nearly skipped through the mall, with the money begging to be spent.

That year a jewelry trend had caught my eye— big gold link-chain necklaces with bracelets and matching earrings. Not usually given to fashion jewelry, I lingered, trying to decide which set to purchase. Meanwhile, the image of a maternity store I'd passed kept coming to mind. A friend of mine was pregnant with her third child and I knew they were really struggling on just one salary.

Before I changed my mind, I marched over to the maternity shop. I bought an anonymous $50 gift certificate and asked them to mail it for me, signing it, "A Love Gift from a Friend."

Two days later, I received a small brown package with a note that said, "Thought you might like these. Found them at a garage sale on Saturday morning for a dollar! Love, Mom." Wrapped in tissue paper was a large gold link-chain necklace with matching bracelet and earrings. God cares about the smallest details.

Then, through a series of miracles, I was the agent for an enormous real estate transaction. Next I was offered a job in a more stable industry. Within six months my debt was paid off and I saved enough money to place a down payment on a house. The property management company that owned the home I rented had declared bankruptcy and I bought it with the help of a partner. In three years my partner's investment was paid off and the trust deed was in my name.

More blessings came, and as I continued to give generously, God showed me that His measuring cup was always bigger than mine.

As I recall the image I saw that morning of mud in the road, I have to smile. I had thought that Jesus would walk through it with me—but He did even more. He lifted me onto His shoulders and carried me above it.

Give, and it will be given to you. A good measure, pressed down, shaken together and running over, will be poured into your lap. For with the measure you use, it will be measured to you. (Luke 6:38)

 Gisele Guilbert is a speaker and consultant who lives on her sailboat in Dana Point Harbor, California with her dog, Mr. Bo. She is currently writing a book titled, *Loving Mom and Dad.* She loves "boat living," especially the opportunities to share her faith with boat slip neighbors. E-mail: giseleg@flash.net

From Worry to Trust

Betty J. Price

What was I going to do? The first of September was only a week away and I hadn't bought one single thing for either of my sons in preparation for the school year. Summer fun had worn holes in the clothes they had worn during the prior school year, and they had outgrown them. Both were also in need of shoes and underwear. As a single parent with limited income, I struggled just to keep the rent paid and food on the table.

I knew I must get some shopping done *soon*. I had procrastinated, knowing that there were almost no funds available for clothes. I began making a list of the items my sons needed for school and the approximate cost. My heart sank when I totaled up the list. I was devastated by the figures. Not in my wildest dreams could I imagine coming up with that kind of money.

I knew crying about my situation would not

bring a solution. The only thing I knew to do was to evaluate the list and whittle it down. Yes, that's what I would do: downsize the list.

But that would have to wait until morning. It was Friday night and my parents had offered to care for the boys so I could attend an Audrey Meier Sing-along with our church's single parent group. All the way home and through the night, a few words Audrey had spoken earlier that evening kept ringing in my ears: "You can't trust and worry at the same time."

Early Saturday morning I got out my list and began crossing off some of the items. I felt tears beginning to swell. Before long, my cheeks were wet as I began to cry softly. I fell to my knees beside my bed and cried out, "Oh, Lord, You know my heart and my desire to put You first in everything I do. I want to believe that You will supply our needs, but it's hard to do and there doesn't seem to be any place to turn. Here's my problem. . . ."

I told Him the whole situation, then I just sat there. I remained motionless for what seemed like an eternity, numbed by my predicament. Suddenly, those words that had haunted me through the night flashed in my mind again: "You can't trust and worry at the same time."

"Oh, Lord," I declared, "I'm deciding right here and now to honor You and to trust You. I'm going to believe Philippians 4:19: 'And my God will meet all your needs according to his glorious riches.' I don't know how You'll do it, but I'm going to trust that You will indeed supply *all* my needs."

Little did I realize, in those moments with God, that an enormous answer to prayer was only a few hours away. After breakfast I told the boys to get ready to go to town. I checked my purse and discovered only one $20 bill. I realized that would permit the purchase of only a few items, but I grabbed the revised list of bare essentials, and the three of us drove downtown.

By some amazing "coincidence" (or better, *answer to prayer*), all the stores were having sidewalk sales—with incredible bargains on clothing. What a delight to find a bin with great shirts for only $1 each! Both boys were able to pick out shirts in their favorite colors. We went from store to store in our buying spree, knowing it would only last as long as the money held out. Within three hours my meager funds were gone.

I had planned to take the boys to the beach as a part of our "outing" that day, but the boys were so excited over their purchases they begged to go home and try on their new clothes. When we got inside the house, we took all the items out of their bags and spread them out on the bed. Then I remembered the original list.

Could this be true? I double-checked the list. It didn't seem possible, but we had actually purchased everything on the original list, including shoes for each of the boys.

I fell to my knees again. This time, my heart was overflowing with thanksgiving that God had so mightly and lovingly supplied our need. This time the tears were of gratitude and joy!

> *Therefore, do not worry, saying, "What shall we eat?" or "What shall we drink?" or "What shall we wear?" . . . For your heavenly Father knows that you need all these things. But seek first the kingdom of God and His righteousness, and all these things shall be added to you. (Matthew 6:31-33, NKJV)*

 Betty J. Price is the author of *101 Ways to Fix Broccoli*. She has also published numerous articles and coauthored with her husband, Harvey, *ABC's of Abundant Living*. In addition to her writing, she has a unique music ministry as a choirchime soloist (an instrument similar to handbells). She lives in San Diego, California.

Chapter 7

Meeting Physical Challenge

He gives strength to the weary and increases the power of the weak. . . . Those who hope in the LORD will renew their strength. (Isaiah 40:29, 31)

I Will Still Praise You

Jo Franz

"Idoubt you will ever sing again."

Those seven words reverberated within my mind. Over and over again they taunted me. The specialist at UCLA Medical Center left me alone in the examining room with tears filling my eyes, stunned by his matter-of-fact statement.

Is this because of sin in my life? A haughty spirit? Have I run ahead of You in ministry and You are slowing me down, Lord? Silent questions arose in my tormented heart. Then, suddenly, peace calmed me as if I'd been soothed by a loving father's hug. That small voice within said, "Trust Me even though you're frightened."

Singing was my life. I had expressed myself through singing since childhood. During college, while on a voice scholarship, I sang in nightclubs.

But when I became a Christian at twenty-three, a new world opened up for me. I proclaimed my love for Jesus through music. When I began giving speaking presentations, I would weave songs with messages into my programs. This ministry had started twenty years ago—shortly before I was diagnosed with multiple sclerosis.

Then on Sunday morning, May 26, 1996, as I spoke with my husband, my voice was suddenly distorted beyond recognition. Ray couldn't understand me! I sounded like I was on a respirator. I couldn't get through a sentence without exhaustion.

Three doctors concurred that MS was attacking nerves in my brain. The nerves weren't getting correct messages to the vocal cords about how to operate. I felt a terror within. An MS attack on my vocal cords? *How will I speak and sing, Lord?*

Melissa, our seventeen-year-old daughter, told me, "Mom, I've been asking God, 'Why her voice, when she reaches so many people for You with her voice?' "

After the specialist informed me I would probably never sing again, I cried unashamedly in the arms of a friend. Then we agreed, "This doctor is not God. He doesn't know the future."

My speech slurred, and I couldn't force words into smooth sentences. I sounded developmentally disabled. It was incredibly humbling. I prayed, "Lord, I don't want to sound like this all my life. Please heal me. But I still want to bring

You glory and honor and praise. I ask for wisdom to see things Your way. Perhaps this is Your will for an indefinite period of time—for *something better.*"

As the months passed, I missed praising God through speaking and singing, so I decided to write. For several years I had dabbled in writing. Now I wanted to get serious. Was this the "something better"?

Reality, on the other hand, didn't feel like something better. One day I cried to my husband, "Don't stop communicating with me! Keep trying. That's a special part of our relationship." Ray learned lipreading and fine-tuned his listening. We avoided restaurant dining for months. Then we picked restaurants according to their loudness, not the ambiance or the food.

Answering the phone was difficult. If people understood me at all, they usually asked why I was depressed or crying. Shopping was the worst. Clerks craned their necks to hear me, strained to read my lips and seemed to wonder if I was "all there." I would stand casually at a counter, smiling to others. When I opened my mouth, countenances changed abruptly. The people stared, then quickly looked away. I felt two inches tall. *Lord, how do I bring You praise when I am like this?*

With each struggle, I turned to God: "Lord, I don't know why my voice must be like this, but I know You have allowed it, and I give thanks to You in it as First Thessalonians 5:18 exhorts.

Teach me as You will. I am reminded: I am to be
for the praise of Your glory."

An offering of praise flowed from my pen:

My voice

not really mine at all
it's Yours to use
to soar in song or
to whisper in darkness.

Even as embarrassed
as I feel at times
I remember
I want to let You shine.

That offering was honored in such a way, I
knew only God could have planned it. A call
from my local MS society chapter provided me a
unique opportunity. The University of California Irvine's theater department was preparing
the play, "Duet for One" about Jacqueline Du-
pree, a famous cellist whose career ended because of MS.

Four people from the theater department
wanted to interview someone who had experienced loss due to MS. After talking for only a few
minutes about my inability to speak and sing, one
asked, "Why aren't you angry or depressed?"

Silently, I thanked God for ordaining that moment. Although I slurred my once-clear words, although I spoke in a monotone where my voice
used to rise and fall naturally and although I whis-

pered with low volume, what I said came through with clarity and power:

"I'm not angry or depressed," I said, "because I have a relationship with God's Son, Jesus Christ. I know He loved me enough to die for me. Since He did that, I know His love won't allow anything to happen to me that He can't use somehow for my good.

"The Bible promises: 'In all things God works for the good of those who love him, who have been called according to his purpose' (Romans 8:28). God has proven Himself to me through many difficult experiences. I'm not saying I don't feel sad or grieve the loss of my voice. But God is trustworthy and I keep coming back to that truth."

For the next two hours those four thespians continued bringing our conversation around to my faith. I counted it an enormous privilege to share about Jesus, and it all happened because of my loss.

Nine months after the MS attack began, I still didn't know if I would ever serve God as I had in the past. My neurologist didn't hold out much hope. Then on Sunday, March 2, 1997, Ray and I drove to Mammoth, in the California Sierras, to go skiing. With the use of outriggers (short skis attached to crutches for balance and braking), I can swish down the slopes. I always thank God for strength to ski and for the sheer joy of feeling graceful on skis, especially since I don't feel graceful walking. I praise Him for His magnificent creation all around me, and I grin from ear to ear. Skiing, for me, is an activity of praise.

As we rode the lift up the mountain, I turned to speak to Ray, leaning over, hoping he could hear me. "I'm so excited to be skiing again!" I said, and then my mouth dropped wide open in amazement! My voice was clear!

All day I kept asking Ray, "Do you hear that? My voice is normal!" My brain had stopped telling the vocal cords to spasm. Wow, did I ever praise God as I skied that day!

Over the months my voice strengthened. It thrilled me to speak and sing again. But what if the Lord hadn't blessed me with the return of my voice? Would I have continued to praise Him? I believe I can heartily answer, Yes! I knew a joy even during those months of suffering and loss. As Job said, "The LORD gave and the LORD has taken away; may the name of the LORD be praised" (Job 1:21).

Shortly after my voice cleared (actually the Lord's voice; it's His to use), I received word that two of my writing projects were successful. God had blessed the time I had spent pursuing a new mode of praising Him. The loss of two loves produced another. Now I speak and sing *and write* for His glory.

O my Strength, I sing praise to you; you, O God, are my fortress, my loving God. (Psalm 59:17)

Jo Franz shares her faith and joy through speaking and singing for retreats, conferences and church events. She has appeared on radio and TV and is a graduate of CLASS (Christian Leaders, Authors and Speakers Seminars). Jo has been published in *Decision* and in *God's Vitamin "C" for the Hurting Spirit*. While freelancing, she is working on her own book. Contact her at P.O. Box 26584, Fresno, CA 93729-6584. E-mail: Jofranz@aol.com

There Is Hope

Terry and Jo Cotter

Part I: Jo's Story

Baseball season was again upon us. It was the spring of 1986, the beginning of what turned out to be a particularly difficult season in my life. I casually listened to an interview of a young Christian ballplayer whose career in the major leagues ended before it had a chance to begin. I didn't listen because I like baseball, but because the battle with infirmity of which the young man spoke was a battle I was also fighting.

I don't recall the name of the ballplayer whose testimony should have prepared me for my own impending battles. I do remember vividly that, for him, baseball was not merely a game; it was a passion. Entering the major leagues was for him the fulfillment of a lifelong dream.

I too was beginning to fulfill my lifetime dream of writing. In August of 1985 I accepted a job with the local newspaper, where I combined my love for writing with my faith. This secular paper was not known for its Christian slant, and I saw my position there as an opportunity to share the good news of Jesus Christ.

Unfortunately, in December of 1985 my health had taken a downward turn. The undiagnosed Epstein-Barr virus left me weak, tired, barely able to get through my part-time hours at the newspaper. I tried to save my job by decreasing my hours, eventually eliminating two days a week from my schedule. These accommodations, however, were not enough. By April I could no longer carry even the reduced schedule. At my boss's request, I obtained paperwork from my physician to hold my position open until I was able to return.

It was just after returning home from delivering the doctor's note to my boss that I tuned in to the ballplayer's testimony. He told how a battle with cancer had threatened to put an end to his promising career. His medical condition worsened, and he prayed for healing, asking God to allow him to return to the game he loved; but in that prayer he placed his life and career in God's care, bowing to heaven's sovereignty in the matter.

No sooner had he finished this prayer, he said, than he received a phone call with the diagnosis that brought his baseball career to a permanent end. From then on his life had taken an entirely different route. Baseball became just a page from his past. Amazingly, he had no regrets.

God was trying to use this testimony to prepare me for what was about to happen in my own life, but at the time I believed my job was secure. I completely missed God in this thing.

A phone call came the next day. The paper could not hold my position open, even with a doctor's note. The loss of my job was devastating. Here I was, doing God's work in a job I was sure He had ordained, doing what I loved most. I couldn't make sense of it.

My health continued to deteriorate. In 1991 I was diagnosed with Chronic Fatigue Immune Dysfunction Syndrome (CFIDS). Only recently, with medications, prayer and the tutelage of the Holy Spirit, has my life begun to turn around.

Restoration, I'm learning, is a process. Too often we expect God to move all at once, and we miss the gradual steps. God usually causes doors to open one at a time. We must go through the first door before He will open the second.

Slowly, those doors are opening for me. God is bringing new people and opportunities into my life. I am once again writing. I have published poetry, am writing and editing a column for a home-school publication and recently received an invitation to contribute to the religion page of the same newspaper that let me go more than ten years ago.

One of the things CFIDS could not rob from me is my marriage. Through months of infections and years of incapacitating fatigue, my husband

Terry remained my friend, my caretaker, my sole support. In my season of suffering he became for me an example of God's love clothed in humanity. Because he was willing to love me when I had nothing to give in return, I am learning to love myself, limitations and all.

The process of healing and restoration continues in my life. I am happy to share that, after years of despair and disappointment, I once again have hope.

Part II: Terry's Story

I was raised to believe that truly successful men do not work for someone else. They make their own way in this world.

Not surprisingly, making money was my primary goal in life. After a few false starts, my landscape/paving company finally took off. I had thirteen men working for me, a yard full of heavy equipment and money in the bank.

Spiritually, I also felt successful. One day I had a vision in which I saw a page turning in a big book. As I watched the page turn I thought, *I've arrived. This is the success for my business. This is the financial prosperity that I have dreamed of. My dreams of money and wealth are about to be fulfilled.*

I was wrong. I misinterpreted the vision. A page was indeed about to turn in my life, but not as I had expected. It was 1990, and everything I had was about to be lost to Chronic Fatigue Immune

Dysfunction Syndrome, the same malady that struck my wife, Jo.

One year later, I was broke. The bank account was drained, the equipment was repossessed, my physical strength was completely zapped. I went from running my own construction company to washing dishes. It was my one job around the house to help out the family, and most of the time I couldn't even do that. Most of my time was spent in bed.

I looked for healing anywhere I could. I hopped on the "name-it-and-claim-it" bandwagon, tacking healing Scriptures up all over the walls and reciting them each morning. I tried treatment with a naturopath (one who relies on natural remedies for healing) and even traveled to a juicing machine presentation during a hurricane. I was desperate to find healing and would go to anyone who promised to help me.

It has been a long, difficult road. I wasn't always faithful to God, bowing willingly to His sovereignty. The truth is, I got angry with God.

But during these seven years, I have gone from spiritual immaturity to growing up in the Lord. I can see how that a richer life than I had before my illness struck awaits me as this maturing process continues in my life. I have learned to be content with little things: sweet peaches and tart apples; the love of my wife; my children; a glowing campfire on a crisp, autumn New England evening.

When Jo and I started out, we were just two people with only one thing in common—God. But

after years of Jo's intercession and love, she fulfilled a part of me that I didn't know was empty.
She's part of me now, and my love for her is
boundless. I look to the future with the great expectation that life will return better than it started.
Like my wife, I too have hope.

*Bless the LORD, O my soul, and forget not all His
benefits: who forgives all your iniquities, who
heals all your diseases. (Psalm 103:2-3, NKJV)*

 Jo and Terry were married in 1981 and
received their call to God's service
shortly thereafter. Because of what they
have endured, they are able to comfort
others—and they do! Contact them by
e-mail at Terry2Jo@aol.com

The Gift

Linda Shepherd

I sat in the stillness of my twenty-one-month-old daughter's hospital room, holding her hand, watching for signs of life. As I studied her, Laura looked as if her dark lashes would flutter open and she would sit up, ending our almost-two-month-long nightmare.

How I longed to hear Laura's giggle as she snuggled with her silky hair against my cheek. I leaned over and kissed her cherubic face. "Honey, it's Mommy. I love you. I know you're in there. I'm waiting—"

The words caught in my throat, and I shut my eyes. If only I could turn back the hand of time and avoid the collision that had saturated our lives with grief.

I remembered sitting in the emergency waiting room with my husband, tearfully waiting for the doctor's verdict.

Paul and I hugged each other and shouted with

joy when the doctor told us, "Laura's going to be all right. Go home and get some rest."

But as I lay on my pillow, I woke up in a cold sweat, picturing the blood that had trickled out of Laura's ear. *Laura is not OK. The crash was too violent. I have to get back to the hospital!*

I raced through the rain-slicked, predawn streets. In Laura's ICU room, I found the staff gathered around her body as it quaked with convulsions.

God, where are You ? I cried like the psalmist.

Three months later, Laura had been moved to another hospital, where she still remained unresponsive. I continued to cry, "Lord, when will You answer my call?"

One evening, as I sat by her bed, listening to the mechanical breathing of her respirator, a strange mood of uncertainty settled over me. I looked at the child I had fought and prayed so hard to keep. *She's really in there, isn't she?*

I stood up, trying to shake the doubt that had suddenly caught me off guard. I decided to get ready for bed. Because Paul was out of town, I wouldn't drive home but would sleep in Laura's room. I shut the door. The nurses had completed their evening rounds. It would be hours before anyone would check on us. I felt alone, too alone. I popped two extra-strength pain relievers and set the bottle on a nearby tray table beside my glass of water. *What if the doctors are right—and Laura never wakes up?* I thought.

Fluffing my pillow, I wondered about God. *Maybe He's abandoned us. Maybe He isn't going to an-*

swer my prayers. I need to face facts: Laura will never awaken. She'll live the rest of her life as a vegetable, hooked to life support.

I tried to stifle my despair, but Laura's respirator seemed to rhythmically mock, *no-hope, no-hope, no-hope.* My chest constricted. Everything suddenly seemed so different, so pointless. *Laura would be better off if she were to die,* I concluded.

I couldn't ask the doctors to take my child off life support after I had already prevented this action once before. But now I accepted that Laura's smile would never return. My dreams for her life were dashed. And God? He had been as silent as Laura's stilled voice.

I was truly alone—miles from my husband, miles from Laura's awareness and light-years from the God I had trusted.

Perhaps God's silence meant I needed to take matters into my own hands. Perhaps it was up to me to end this horrible suffering.

I can turn off the alarms and unplug the respirator from the wall. It would be so simple, except—except, I wondered, *if I kill my daughter, how can I live with myself?*

I found myself staring at my bottle of painkillers. *If I swallowed them . . . no one would find us until morning. . . . Laura and I could . . . escape . . . this living hell . . . together.*

Just as my plan seemed like the only solution, I found my hand resting on my belly. My hidden child was only two weeks old, but I knew he was there.

My mind cleared. How could I kill myself? How could I kill Laura? A new life was growing inside me. A life that had the right to live!

My perspective returned. *Lord, I'm willing to wait—despite the pain and the cost. I'm willing to wait on You.*

The word *wait* brought Isaiah 40:31 into my consciousness. "They that wait upon the LORD shall renew their strength; they shall mount up with wings as eagles; they shall run, and not be weary; and they shall walk, and not faint" (KJV).

I cried myself to sleep. Nine months later, my daughter began to emerge from her coma just before her baby brother, Jimmy, was born.

Although her eyes fluttered open, her gaze was fixed. She remained hooked to life support and slumped in her wheelchair, totally paralyzed. But though she was diagnosed as blind, her eyes began to focus once again.

What's the most important gift a person can give? My daughter gives it often, even though she has to sit in a wheelchair and does not have the ability to speak. I think the gift of love Laura so freely gives is worth more than any other gift that even an able-bodied person can offer.

Although I still sometimes weep over the Laura I have lost, I embrace the Laura who has returned. Recently, when she and Jimmy were baptized, at their requests, the tears in my eyes were not from sorrow, but from joy. How glad I am that I waited on God.

I still face obstacles. But God enables me to run

the race set before me, a race I now know I can finish.

Excerpted and abridged from Faith Never Shrinks in Hot Water, *Copyright 1996 by Linda Shepherd.*

Linda Evans Shepherd, the 1997 Colorado Christian Author of the Year, speaks at retreats and conferences around the country. She is the author of ten books, including her latest, *Love's Little Recipes for Life.* She is a member of National Speakers Association and was trained by CLASS (Christian Leaders, Authors and Speakers Seminars). Fax (303) 678-0260 or e-mail Lswrites@aol.com

But I Know Who
Takes Care of Lives

Vincent Kituku

"My children, I would like to tell you what the doctors have said. . . ." A very long pause. "They can say anything, but *I know who takes care of lives.*"

That is how my mother, Margaret Kasiva, started and ended the news that she had countable days left to live. It was in 1984, and the thought that her days were numbered was the heaviest burden I had carried for many years.

That was in 1984. Three years earlier, in 1981, my mother had given birth to her last child—a son. Two weeks later, they operated on him and found the baby had been born without a liver. It had been destroyed by cancer. He died a few hours after the operation. The doctor recommended that my mother be checked immediately.

Now, in 1984, my wife and I were working in one of my father's coffee gardens. My mother joined us there at about noon and broke the news. Doctors had found that she had uterine cancer. They had also indicated that it was terminal in nature. But she ended this news by saying, "They can say anything, but I know who takes care of lives."

As the firstborn, I believe my mother was telling me this so that I could take care of my young brothers and sisters. The thought of my mother not being alive was devastating.

Our family structure had changed in the early '70s when my father became a polygamist—having more than one wife concurrently, not consecutively. The emotional drain on our family was traumatic.

One day I asked Mom whether it was a must for us to go through what we were experiencing. Her response was, "My son, if it were not for you, my children, I wouldn't." There were eight of us altogether at that time, and divorce was not common. There would be no support for our schooling if my mother chose to leave and take us.

My mother became my friend, mentor on life ethics, a constant example of a living sacrifice for the future of her offspring and an ever-present source of inspiration. Ever since those tough and tender days, I had only one prayer: *God, keep my mother alive.* I wanted to make her happy and let her know that her endurance was not in vain.

So the news from the doctor was a major blow.

I had a year left before I graduated from college. Well, God's ways are above our ways. Although I had not accepted Jesus Christ as my personal Savior at the time my mother learned about her condition, she had taken me to church when I was young and taught me the importance of praying. So I started praying for her immediately. Soon after that, I came to know Jesus as my personal Savior. I prayed for my wife's salvation and my mother's healing.

My mother's condition brought spiritual landmarks in my life. I learned to trust God even while hoping. My first lesson, Isaiah 43:2, "When thou passest through the waters, I will be with thee; and through the rivers, they shall not overflow thee: when thou walkest through the fire, thou shalt not be burned; neither shall the flame kindle upon thee" (KJV). The word "when" (not "in case" or "if") taught me that adversities in life are inevitable. The word "will" affirmatively indicates God's promise of His presence during the tough times.

I fasted for the first time in my life to seek God's will in my mother's condition. During my fasting time, I learned "Amazing Grace" by heart and learned the importance of initial response. How we first respond when faced with adversity and our attitude during the ordeal are closely related to the outcome.

The Bible tells us that when Job saw all that was happening to him, instead of laying down strategies on how to recover his wealth and children, he worshiped and trusted God. In the same way, mother said, "But I know who takes care of lives."

My graduation came. I was able to go to the United States for further studies, and while at the University of Wyoming, I began to attend a church that believed in divine healing. As an indication that they were trusting God for someone's healing, they would send a handkerchief to such an individual in a manner similar to the apostle Paul in Acts 19:12. In 1987 I sent my mother one. I explained to her that handkerchiefs do not heal anybody. It was merely a tangible indication that I, and other God-loving people, were praying for her healing.

Unknown to me, my mother took that handkerchief with childlike faith and *slept* on it at night! About a year later, I suddenly remembered that I had not heard whether my mother was going for a checkup, although we were communicating every month. I called her and asked how she was doing. She said, "You know, ever since you sent that handkerchief to me, I have never felt sick. In fact I did go for a checkup and they found nothing wrong with me."

Hallelujah!! Amen. The God "who takes care of lives," really took care of her.

After this I desperately wanted to see my mother. I couldn't figure how to get her over to the U.S., given the travel costs from Africa to Boise, Idaho. Then, in 1996, I wrote a motivational book of African folktales. It was in both English and Kikamba so my mother would be able to read what she had passed on to me.

When the book came out, I prayed a simple prayer, "God, if You will make this book sell well, I will be able to pay for my mother's airline ticket to visit us in Boise, Idaho." Within weeks after its printing, I had enough money for my mother to come.

On May 11, 1996, I saw my mother, friend and mentor. She saw two of her grandchildren whom she had not seen before. Our last child, our only boy, was born while she was with us here. After my mother returned to Kenya, I wrote a long poem (my very first poem) for her. Here's part of it:

You taught me that life storms are but for a brief season.
You said there is always a rainbow behind every cloud
and a stream in every desert of life.
You said there is always a mountain peak
behind every deep, deep valley of life.
You said there is always a human soul in every person.
You said there is always God in life.

 Dr. Vincent Kituku is an author, motivational speaker, storyteller and seminar leader. He inspires people to identify and face their problems, accept change as a way of life and hold the light high for others. He interweaves modern institutional knowledge and life experience with African cultural wisdom to address the challenges of individuals and of organizations. Contact him at P.O. Box 7152, Boise, ID 83707 or by e-mail at MKMUSOO@aol.com

One Day at a Time!

Dianne McGarey

*W*hen Mom broke the news about my younger brother, there was fear in her voice. "The doctor thinks it could be a bad infection, or . . ."

"Or what?" I said.

I hung up the phone, and time stood still for me. How could I wait three days to find out if my brother had *cancer*? This was the guy who set an all-time forty-seven-point school record during his senior year on the basketball team, the guy who graduated magna cum laude from Georgia Tech and went on to earn his MBA at Dartmouth! At the age of twenty-eight, he was just beginning to fly in a new, high-tech career.

It had to be an infection of some sort. I wouldn't let myself believe otherwise. My husband, Tom, and I prayed that night like never before.

By Monday afternoon I was engrossed in business as usual at the office. At 3 p.m. my secretary announced a call for me, saying, "It's your mom." I flew to the phone and heard a carefully controlled voice at the other end of the line.

"They think it's Hodgkins," she said, "There are more tests to do before they can be sure. The doctor says that Hodgkins is treatable and that chances are good for total recovery."

Hot tears flowed down my face. My coworkers gathered around my desk. As the owner and president of a small company, I had always been able to put up a good front for my employees, but this was one time I had to lean on them. Thank God they were all Christians and promised to pray faithfully during the ordeal to follow.

I learned that the prognosis was not quite as bright as we had hoped. Jim was in the fourth (and final) stage of large-cell lymphoma, which is fatal in eighty percent of the cases studied. The doctor told us the cancer treatment would take from six to nine months, during which time Jim would be unable to work. He was firm in his recommendation that aggressive treatment begin immediately.

Jim went for the bottom line as he questioned the doctor: "What are my chances?"

"Fifty-fifty," said the doctor.

"That's good enough for me. Let's get started!" Jim said.

The treatments were not bad at first. Jim was an athlete and had never abused his body with alcohol, cigarettes or drugs. His faith was strong and, from the beginning, he let us know that he was not afraid to die. We had daily devotionals and prayer as a family unit in addition to individual time with the Lord.

I thought over and over again, *If I ever had a mustard seed's worth of faith, now's the time to use it!* It was too scary to look into the future, so I determined to live and pray one day at a time—thankful for every minute of life we had with Jim.

The treatments became harder after three months. Jim lost his hair and muscle mass in his arms and legs. Between treatments every two weeks, there were only two or three days when he felt well enough to get out of bed. On those days we would pack a picnic lunch and go to a nearby river park to let Jim drink in the fresh air and sunshine.

Our family enlisted prayer support from six different churches, and the cards and letters flowed. I never understood until then how important prayer really was! I've prayed for others who were sick— but when your own family is involved, there is a greater sense of urgency.

My mother saved every card expressing the love and prayers of our friends and church family. We read them over and over for hope and the affirmation that we were not fighting this battle alone.

Jim's tumor, which had started in his spleen, had spread up and down his spine and into the lymph nodes. With every treatment the cancer abated dramatically. After the first three months of progress, we became confident of his recovery.

However, over time Jim became sicker from the treatments. He clung to the hope that after six months this torture would be over.

On the day of the six-month CAT scan we were all set for a victory. The doctor studied the scans carefully, then said, "The spleen is still not completely clear. I'm sorry to tell you this, but I've got to order three more months of treatment."

Jim's head fell to his hands. Tears came to his eyes. Not since the original diagnoses had we felt so defeated. Each of us dealt with that blow in a different way. Jim went to his room and just wanted to be alone. It was quiet in the house, but the prayers continued.

At the end of the eighth month, Jim got the call he'd been waiting for. The CAT scan showed only a small dot in his spleen where the tumor had started. Tom treated us all to a wonderful "victory supper" that night and there were tears of joy and prayers of thanksgiving all around.

The next morning, as Jim came down the stairs I looked up to see the face of a young man who had fought—and won—the greatest battle of his life. His hair would soon grow back, and his body would heal from the ravages of chemotherapy. He grinned that boyish grin I remembered from his childhood and gave me a hug that lasted a long time.

I blinked back tears of relief, thinking back over the intensity of the last eight months. A warm glow filled the room, and I promised myself I would never forget to live in the present, one day at a time, because—that's where God is!

"Therefore do not worry about tomorrow, for tomorrow will worry about itself. Each day has enough trouble of its own." (Matthew 6:34)

Dianne McGarey and her husband, Tom, live in Atlanta, Georgia, where she is a Meeting and Corporate Event Planner. She is active in the women's ministry of Peachtree Corners Baptist Church and enjoys speaking and sharing her testimony of how God has worked in her life. Fax (770) 840-9541 or phone (770) 447-6136.

Do You Want to Be Well?

Bruce Larson

Our expectations are a powerful shaping force in all the areas of our lives, particularly our health. That's why the question we'll be considering here is so pertinent. It was addressed to a paralyzed man who had been an invalid for thirty-eight years. (See John 5:1-15.)

The question Jesus put to the paralyzed man seems an odd one: "Do you want to be well?"

But let's examine the setting in which this was asked.

Jesus was strolling by the pool of Bethesda, a pool known for its healing properties. People with all sorts of diseases gathered there because it was believed that from time to time an angel troubled the waters. When that happened, the first person in received healing.

We might at first consider this belief somewhat

195

primitive, but we still have healing shrines today, including the famous one at Lourdes. People visit those places expecting a miracle. Some receive one, it would seem, and some do not, for reasons we can't explain.

In answer to Jesus' question, the paralyzed man protested that he was a victim of the carelessness or indifference or inefficiency of family or friends. In thirty-eight years they had never gotten him into the pool in time. But he must have indicated his willingness to be healed, for Jesus said, "Take up your bed and walk." The man did so.

The story is intriguing and a source of great hope for all of us. In the case of this man who had been afflicted for so long, there was no attempt to review either his worthiness or his faith. Did he deserve God's special attention? It is not even an issue. The man needed only to be willing. Jesus demonstrated not only His love but His eagerness to bring restoration and health.

"Do you want to be well?" From that one question we could write a whole theology of grace. God is not just our Creator and our Redeemer. He wants to release His power into our lives and make us whole, but we need to be willing.

The paralytic's response to Jesus' question strikes a familiar note. Offered healing by this strange prophet he does not know, he gives an answer that sounds defensive. Rather than replying with a straight yes or no, he indicates that his condition is not his fault. His friends and family have failed him.

His answer, you'll notice, has nothing to do with the question asked. He implies, as Adam and Cain did, that he is a victim in life and, further, that he is unloved and uncared-for.

God wants to give us wellness or wholeness, to make us what we are meant to be. But we are such defensive, guilt-ridden, complicated people that we cannot respond easily to God's simple offer.

Jesus is still asking us, "Do you want to be well?" Does the question seem odd? Would someone who is sick physically or morally or spiritually or mentally or relationally not want to be well?

The unspoken message in Jesus' question is that we sometimes must pay a price to be well. We may refuse to choose wellness because of the benefits of having an illness. The man by the pool of Bethesda did not have to work. Somebody carried him down to the pool each day, where he could lie in the shade and hear all the local gossip.

I broke my leg once in a skiing accident. I traveled the country for six weeks with it in a cast, keeping my speaking engagements. My situation had real perks. The airlines arranged to drive me from plane to plane; I got to board first and was given a desirable seat. But best of all, all my failures were forgiven.

If the speech was not my best, or even if I bombed out, people were kind. Invariably someone would say, "Aren't you wonderful to come here and stand on that broken leg and speak to us!" I found my handicap to be an advantage, and that could have become addictive.

We may avoid God's question, believing that we are powerless to help ourselves. The man by the pool implied that he was powerless, and that is a myth for any of us. Everybody has some degree of power and can choose to use it.

Some years ago I visited a doctor for a thorough checkup. After endless tests, the great man received me, examined all my charts and pronounced me reasonably well for a man my age. Glancing at the record of my weight, he asked me a surprising question: "What do you want to weigh?"

I was caught off guard. I felt like saying, "What do I want to weigh? You're the doctor; you tell me what I should weigh."

Then it dawned on me that he was smart enough not to make my weight his problem. I stammeringly told him I wanted to weigh maybe ten, fifteen pounds less, and he said, "I'd like to help you with that." He came on board as my partner, not as a taskmaster with whom I could engage in a continuing struggle about my weight.

The myth of powerlessness has permeated so many areas of life in these last years. Do you want to be well? Do you want the love and joy and peace that God offers? Having been given free will, we have the option of saying no. God will not force His health, His life, His kingdom, His life-style on anyone. It is a choice.

I have an old friend named Ernie who was for many years the pastor of a church in the heart of Baltimore. One Sunday he preached on that well-known text from Romans 8:28: "And we know that in all things God works for the good of those who love him, who have been called according to his purpose."

Later, while he stood at the door shaking hands, a man he had not seen before came up, looked him in the eye, and said, "Pastor, do you believe what you were preaching this morning?" Ernie was startled.

"I've never been asked that question before," he said. "Let me think about it." But just seconds later, he said, "Yes, yes, I really believe that with all my heart."

The very next day Ernie went duck hunting on Chesapeake Bay with some men from his parish. On the way to the duck blind, one of his companions tripped. His shotgun went off and blew out Ernie's eyes. He has been blind ever since.

I met him after that accident. He traveled up and down the East Coast to conferences with his Seeing Eye dog. I have never known a man more full of joy and love and faith and optimism than Ernie.

On one occasion he told me, "Bruce, my church is in revival. More people are coming, more people are accepting Jesus Christ, and one of the best things is my counseling ministry. I see people who would never come to me if I had sight because they'd be ashamed to be recognized on the street. They can unburden their secret safely with a blind man. My ministry is being blessed because of my blindness."

Being well presupposes that we are free from addictions, that we are able to give and receive love, that we are functioning adequately at home and at work and that we are pursuing healthy relationships. In short, it means being all that God has in mind for us.

During a research project more than a decade ago, I spent some time with the staff at the Menninger Clinic. One of the questions I asked was if they could pinpoint the single most important ingredient in healing. The answer: hope—hope that you are not a prisoner of your track record, that you don't have to be what you have always been, that tomorrow is going to be better than today.

Excerpted and abridged from What God Wants to Know (Finding Your Answers in God's Vital Questions) *by Bruce Larson, Copyright 1993, Harper, San Francisco. Used by permission.*

Dr. Bruce Larson received his Master of Divinity from Princeton Theological Seminary and M.A. in Psychology from Boston University. He also holds LL.D. and D.D. degrees. He is the author of twenty-three books. There are over 3 million copies of his books in print, not including translations in several foreign languages. He has served as Senior Pastor of the University Presbyterian Church in Seattle, Washington for ten years and is currently Pastor Emeritus there. Dr. Larson and his wife, Hazel, who is also his primary editor, live in Washington, near Seattle.

Chapter 8

The Healing Balm of Forgiveness

Let all bitterness and wrath and anger and clamor and slander be put away from you, with all malice, and be kind to one another, tenderhearted, forgiving one another, as God in Christ forgave you. (Ephesians 4:31-32, RSV)

The Servant
As a Forgiver

Charles R. Swindoll

orgiveness is not an elective in the curriculum of servanthood. It is a required course, and the exams are always tough to pass.

Several years ago I was in search of a pastoral intern. In the process of interviewing a number of men, I met a seminarian I will never forget. I was extremely impressed with his sensitivity to God. It was obvious that the Lord was deeply at work in his life. The marks of a servant's heart were clearly visible, so much so that I probed to discover why. Among other things he related an incredible, true story that illustrated how God was molding him and shaping him through one of those tough "forgiveness exams." As best as I can remember, here's his story. I'll call him Aaron, not his real name.

Late one spring Aaron was praying about having a significant ministry the following summer. He asked God for a position to open up on some church staff or Christian organization. Nothing happened. Summer arrived, still nothing. Aaron finally faced reality—he needed *any* job he could find. The only thing that seemed a possibility was driving a bus in southside Chicago . . . nothing to brag about, but it would help with tuition in the fall. After learning the route, he was on his own— a rookie driver in a dangerous section of the city. It wasn't long before Aaron realized just *how* dangerous his job really was.

A gang of tough kids spotted the young driver and began to take advantage of him. For several mornings in a row they got on, walked right past him without paying, ignored his warnings and rode until they decided to get off . . . all the while making smart remarks to him and others on the bus. Finally, he decided that had gone on long enough.

The next morning, after the gang got on as usual, Aaron saw a policeman on the next corner, so he pulled over and reported the offense. The officer told them to pay or get off. They paid . . . but, unfortunately, the policeman got off. And they stayed on. When the bus turned another corner or two, the gang assaulted the young driver.

When he came to, blood was all over his shirt, two teeth were missing, both eyes were swollen, his money was gone and the bus was empty. Resentful thoughts swarmed his mind. Confusion,

anger and disillusionment added fuel to the fire of
his physical pain. He spent a fitful night wrestling
with his Lord.

*How can this be? Where's God in all of this? I genu-
inely want to serve Him. I prayed for a ministry. I was
willing to serve Him anywhere doing anything . . . and
this is the thanks I get!*

Aaron decided to press charges. With the help
of the police officer and several who were willing
to testify as witnesses, most of the gang were
rounded up and taken to the local county jail.
Within a few days there was a hearing before a
judge.

In walked Aaron and his attorney plus the angry gang members who glared across the room in
his direction. Suddenly he was seized with a
whole new series of thoughts. Not bitter ones, but
compassionate ones! His heart went out to the
guys who had attacked him. Under the Spirit's
control he no longer hated them—he pitied them.
They needed help, not more hate. What could he
do? Or say?

Suddenly, after there had been a plea of guilty,
Aaron (to the surprise of his attorney and everybody else in the courtroom) stood to his feet and
requested permission to speak.

"Your honor, I would like you to total up all the
days of punishment against these men—all the
time sentenced against them—and I request that
you allow me to go to jail in their place."

Both attorneys were stunned. As Aaron looked
over at the gang members (whose mouths and

eyes looked like saucers), he smiled and said quietly, "It's because I forgive you."

The dumbfounded judge, when he reached a level of composure, said rather firmly: "Young man, you're out of order. This sort of thing has never been done before!" To which the young man replied with genius insight:

"Oh, yes, it has, your honor . . . yes, it has. It happened over nineteen centuries ago when a man from Galilee paid the penalty that all mankind deserved."

And then, for the next three or four minutes, without interruption, he explained how Jesus Christ died on our behalf, thereby proving God's love and forgiveness.

He was not granted his request, but the young man visited the gang members in jail, led most of them to faith in Christ and began a significant ministry to many others in Southside Chicago.

He passed a tough exam. And, as a result, a large door of ministry—the very thing he'd prayed for—opened up before him.

Through the pain of abuse and assault, Aaron began to get a handle on serving others.

Forgiving (like giving) improves our serve.

Excerpted and abridged from Improving Your Serve, *Charles R. Swindoll. Copyright 1981, Word Publishers, Nashville, Tennessee. All rights reserved.*

Remember, the Lord forgave you, so you must forgive others. (Colossians 3:13, TLB)

Dr. Charles R. Swindoll was the Senior Pastor of the First Evangelical Free Church of Fullerton, California for twenty-eight years. He currently lives in Dallas, Texas where he is the President of Dallas Theological Seminary. He is author of numerous best-selling books, and is nationally and internationally known through his radio ministry, *Insight For Living*, a thirty-minute broadcast heard over 200 times every day.

"You'd Better Be Good!"

Marlene Bagnull

Sunday's paper was fat with ads for last-minute Christmas shoppers. Big, bold letters warned there were only a few days left to buy gifts for loved ones. *And to get everything else done*, I thought grimly. But it wasn't just time pressures that were getting to me. It was everything.

I remembered my childhood, how my mother used to get irritable as the holidays approached. "I'd like to forget all about Christmas," she'd grumble.

I thought she was awful for feeling that way. Now I had become just like her.

"Oh, God, what's wrong with me?" I wept. "I should be happy. You've blessed me with a good husband and beautiful children. We're healthy. We have a nice home. We've seen You working in our lives this past year."

I knew I should go on to list our many, many blessings; but other emotions that were too powerful to suppress kept surfacing. Anger, hurt, guilt. No matter how hard I tried, I felt I would never be able to measure up to what God and others expected of me. For some reason the coming of Christmas intensified those feelings.

My eye caught the words at the top of an advertisement: "Toys for good girls and boys."

Suddenly a torrent of painful, buried memories flooded over me. "Santa won't come if you're not a good girl," my mother and father began threatening as soon as the stores decorated for Christmas.

I'd try, really try, to be good, but I never felt I was good enough. On Christmas Eve I would go to bed filled with fear that there would be only coal in my stocking the next morning.

I remembered getting walking dolls and a train set, but I couldn't remember ever feeling that they gave me those gifts because they loved me. I couldn't remember being hugged—especially by my father.

What I did remember were his slaps across my face and the way he locked me in his bedroom. (I didn't have a room of my own.) I cried alone for hours before he finally opened the door. When he did, he never told me it was OK now. He never told me that he forgave me—that he loved me.

I wanted to push the memories back down inside, but God wouldn't let me. "It's time for you to be free of them," He gently said.

"But how, Lord?" I wept.

"Can you forgive him?" He asked.

"I don't know," I replied, realizing how those childhood experiences had shaped my entire life. No wonder I felt anger, hurt and guilt. For years I had been trying to be good enough to make people love me—to make God love me. But I had never made it—and never would.

"Nor do you have to, My child," I felt Him say. "You don't have to earn My love. It's My Christmas gift to you."

"But I can't give You anything, Lord. I can't even live the way You want me to live. I fail You so miserably."

"No, those are lies you've been believing for too long. Listen to My words of truth."

What was truth? I thought. *Did my father ever love me?* I'd never know. He died when I was twelve. As far as I knew, he never accepted the Lord. I didn't dare to hope I'd someday see him in heaven.

My father had been seriously ill most of my life. He was hospitalized more times than I could remember with insulin shock, heart trouble, a collapsed lung. I was never allowed to visit him.

When he came home, I had to be super-good. Especially the time he had a blood clot in his leg. My mother warned me that if I wasn't good, if I got him upset, the blood clot could go to his heart and kill him.

The truth. Suddenly I saw it. *I* wasn't the problem! His health was the problem. I probably wasn't any more naughty than any other child. They were just under so much stress. They didn't mean to hurt me. They didn't mean to withhold their love.

And, I realized, I couldn't continue to withhold my love—my forgiveness.

"God, I want to be free," I prayed. "Help me forgive him and Mother too. Take away the anger that has been festering in me for so long, and the hurt, the guilt."

I felt God performing surgery on my soul. I knew I'd never again need to be driven by those "you'd better be good" threats. I had received the best Christmas gift possible. God loved me so much that He sent His only Son to die on the cross for my sins. He had forgiven me for every time I failed Him. And He would keep me from "slipping and falling away" and bring me, "sinless and perfect, into his glorious presence with mighty shouts of everlasting joy" (Jude 1:25, TLB).

 Marlene Bagnull authored her fifth book in 1997. She is director of the Colorado and Greater Philadelphia Christian Conferences. She has written for numerous Christian periodicals and is a frequent speaker at Christian writers' conferences around the nation. She lives in Drexel Hill, Pennsylvania. Visit her webpage at http://nancepub.com/cwf/

Grace on a Saturday Afternoon

Beverly Bush Smith

The sun shone warm and bright, but a cool breeze blew from the ocean through the hills. As I pushed my sixteen-month-old grandson, Trevor, up one of the hills in his jogging stroller, I sang, "Jesus loves you, this I know."

When we reached the brow of the hill, I peeked around at him and saw he'd slipped down in his seat. Slipping the safety strap from my wrist, I walked around the stroller and repositioned him. At that moment the ferns of wild fennel growing at the side of the street caught my eye. I'd pluck a bit and tickle Trevor, I decided. I leaned over to break off a sprig. "Look, Trevor!"

But Trevor wasn't there. As I turned, I saw to my horror the stroller rolling backward down the steep hill, gaining momentum. I started to run,

but I knew I couldn't reach it before it smashed
into the bumper of a parked car. The stroller hit
the car with a sickening clang of metal, capsized
sideways, and Trevor's screams echoed through
the hills.

"Oh, God, no!" I cried.

Heart pounding with terror, I righted the
stroller and, with trembling hands, examined
Trevor's head, arms and legs. No visible injuries,
thank God, and he was certainly having no
trouble flailing his arms and legs. Carefully, I un-
belted him and picked him up, cradling him close,
longing to comfort and reassure him. I wept aloud,
"Oh, Lord, please, please, please! He's the most
precious being in my whole world!"

Trevor clung to me while I ached for my viola-
tion of his trust. *How could I have been so stupid?* I
berated myself. The stroller had only a small hand
brake. Oh, why hadn't I kept the safety strap
around my wrist? If he wasn't all right, could I
ever forgive myself? Could my son, Bryan, and
his wife, Linda, ever forgive me?

Gradually, Trevor quieted. But was he all
right? He could have a head injury. Should I look
for an emergency medical facility nearby and have
him checked? I had no car, and my husband,
Bryan and Linda all were ten miles away, working
in the house they'd just bought, which didn't yet
have a phone.

Trevor's condition didn't seem to warrant a 911
call, but I didn't want him to go to sleep till I was
sure he was all right, so I wheeled him to the park.

When I lifted him from the stroller, he stood beside it for a long time. I checked him over from head to toe. Not a scratch, lump or bump. At last he ventured toward the fence to watch the Little League game in progress.

My heart was still beating furiously as I watched for any symptoms of head injury. But he seemed normal. By the time we went back to the house, an hour later, a telltale red mark had appeared on his cheek. Nothing more.

Oh, Lord, I prayed, *Thank You. Thank You for saving my Trevor. I confess, I'm guilty of . . .* I struggled to name it—child neglect! *I don't deserve ever to take care of my grandson again. He's not safe with me. Linda and Bryan will never trust him to me again—and rightly so. Oh, Lord, forgive me!*

I sat envisioning Linda and Bryan chastising me and my husband asking, "What were you thinking of?" They'd all judge me incompetent and they'd be right. It was only by the grace of God that Trevor had survived and that he wasn't even injured.

"The grace of God!" I exclaimed aloud. "That's what it's all about!" If the definition of grace is "unmerited favor," surely I had experienced it. I'd been irresponsible—at what could have been terrible cost. Yet God had spared both Trevor—and me.

"Lord," I wept, "You are a God of grace and mercy. You placed Your guardian angels around my precious grandson and protected him. Thank You, thank You!"

Now I needed to confess my negligence—first

to Linda, who came home first, then to Bryan.
Linda's response astonished me. "Are you all
right?" she asked.

Bryan—in that amazing way men have of fo-
cusing on the technical—puzzled, "The stroller
capsized. That's interesting." But he didn't chas-
tise me, either. Nor did my husband. Grace and
more grace.

That night, I crept into Trevor's room repeatedly to check on him, each time finding him
breathing and sleeping peacefully.

Back in bed, as I replayed the day's events, I felt
myself falling into a pit of guilt and failure. I wept
hot tears of self-condemnation and blame onto my
pillow. Then, all at once, I remembered that I had
confessed my sin to the Lord, and that God, in
His grace (that word again!), promises to cleanse
me of all unrighteousness. Moreover, He promises
He will remember my sin no more. And I realized
that even if Linda and Bryan hadn't forgiven me,
God would, and He *had*.

As I continued meditating, I remembered God's
promise that His grace is, as Paul wrote in Second
Corinthians 12:9, "sufficient for you, for my
power is made perfect in weakness" (RSV). His
grace had been sufficient not only to spare Trevor
and to bring me through this trauma, but to restore me to serve Him and my family.

Then I wondered: Would His grace have been
sufficient if Trevor had been severely injured or—
I could hardly bear to think the thought—if he'd
died?

I could hear my own heartbeat, and at last, in the dark, I found my Bible and tiptoed into the bathroom to consult my concordance. And there, under "grace," I found Hebrews 4:16: "Let us then approach the throne of grace with confidence, so that we may receive mercy and find grace to help us in our time of need."

I reread the verse, turned off the light and stole back to bed. The throne of grace. Yes, I could approach it with confidence. It was then I remembered a friend who had struck and killed a child in an automobile accident. In time, she had experienced that mercy and grace. I drifted off to sleep singing praise songs in my head.

When I awoke the next morning, I opened my Bible once again and God showed me yet another Scripture on grace: "See to it that no one misses the grace of God" (Hebrews 12:15).

And so at breakfast I shared with my unbelieving family: husband, son and daughter-in-law, how the entire episode illuminated the magnitude of God's grace. We all looked at Trevor, bouncing in his high chair, jabbering a stream of chatter welcome to my ears. And my daughter-in-law, eyes bright with tears, reached over to touch Trevor's cheek and whispered, "Thank You, God!"

Later that morning, as my son and husband left to work on the new house, my daughter-in-law asked, "Are you OK to stay with Trevor?"

I hesitated for a moment. "Yes, but are you OK for me to stay with him?"

"Of course," she said. "Take him out for a good long walk."

Grateful for her confidence, I wondered nonetheless if my grandson would remember and recoil from the stroller when I took him out that morning.

He appeared to have forgotten the incident, snuggling into the stroller as I belted him in. And as I gazed into his wide blue eyes, full of love and trust, my own eyes filled with tears as I saw this human reflection of God's forgiveness.

I, even I, am he who blots out your transgressions, for my own sake, and remembers your sins no more. (Isaiah 43:25)

Beverly Bush Smith is the author of two novels; coauthor of three nonfiction books, *Uniquely You, Change for the Better* and *Caught in the Middle;* and has published more than 500 articles. She leads Bible studies, mentors a MOPS (Mothers of Preschoolers) group and speaks to women's groups. Fax her at (714) 458-8981 or write to her at 24302 Ontario Lane, Lake Forest, CA 92630.

Bricks in Your Backpack

Zig Ziglar

While the following is not primarily a personal experience story, its message of forgiveness is, nevertheless, a key to "bouncing back" from broken relationships. Forgiveness can heal past hurts, erase resentments, resolve old grudges and restore healthy and caring friendships. It also helps us to experience more fully the joy of God's presence and the abundant life He offers us.—DLJ

It is safe to say that in a lifetime, all of us have what we consider to be more than our share of ups and downs. In that sense, life truly is a roller coaster. Sometimes things happen to us that are genuine accidents; sometimes we sabotage ourselves and are our own worst enemies. On occasion people or life itself deals us a series of body blows that devastate us.

For some of you, the hurts are too many and

too deep, and they did too much damage—or at any rate, that is your feeling, and you will probably need counseling to steer you through the pain and into the channel of forgiveness. I encourage you to get that help because you must—repeat *must*—forgive that person. The commandment to forgive does not include any exceptions.

Several years ago in a conference I heard one of the most moving testimonials as it relates to the peace and power that go with forgiveness that I've ever heard. A strong man, very successful in business, was telling about his experiences as a child with his father. Soon after his birth, his father went off to war, and the first four years of his life he seldom saw his dad. His mother and grandmother were his primary caregivers. When Dad returned home, he quickly observed that "those women" had "ruined his son," and he was "going to make a man of him."

His dad was a strict and harsh disciplinarian. Once, as a six-year-old on his way home from school, the boy was accosted by a bully who proceeded to beat him up. He ran home crying, and his dad told him that as long as he was acting like a girl he would dress him like one. He put a dress on the little boy and sent him back to face the bully.

As the successful businessman sat there with tears streaming down his cheeks, he said that was one of the reasons he had emotional difficulties in his life, including becoming an alcoholic. However, he said he realized through working through

an alcoholic recovery program that his dad did not
treat him that way because he hated him; he
treated him that way because he loved him. That
was the way his dad had been raised, and that was
the only way he knew how to deal with problems
of that nature. He pointed out that once he understood why his dad did what he did, he was able to
forgive him and get on with his life.

Many of you who read these words may have
been mistreated or abused. Forgive the person
who abused you. You might well rationalize that
the person doesn't deserve forgiveness. I encourage you to leave that up to God; let Him be the
decider of who deserves and who does not deserve
forgiveness.

Just as mountain climbers don't add bricks to
their backpacks, through forgiveness you will remove the bricks of anger, hate and resentment.
Your load will be lighter; you can move forward
and upward much faster. Through the process of
forgiving you will make friends with the past and
be able to focus on the present. This gives you the
freedom to grow and become the person you are
capable of becoming.

If you had a broken leg you would not hesitate
to seek professional help. I encourage you to seek
professional counseling and seek a counselor who
will give that counseling based on biblical principles.

Actually, you have the services of the most capable counselor in town at your disposal. The
charge is zero; He's available twenty-four hours a

day; and He has plenty of time to listen and give advice. If you get tired of talking, you can read His book. Bible reading is a tremendous confidence builder. It's exciting to know that 365 different times in the Bible you are told to "fear not." There is one "fear not" for every day in the year except leap year—and surely you can get through that day. Just in case you can't, God is always open for business, even on that extra day.

You are at the top when . . .

- You have made friends with your past, and you are focused on the present and optimistic about your future.
- You love the unlovable, give hope to the hopeless, friendship to the friendless and encouragement to the discouraged.
- You can look back in forgiveness, forward in hope, down in compassion and up with gratitude.
- You clearly understand that yesterday ended last night and today is a brand-new day—and it's yours.
- You are pleasant to the grouch, courteous to the rude and generous to the needy.
- You stand in front of the Creator of the universe, and He says to you, "Well done, thou good and faithful servant."

Excerpted and abridged from Over the Top, *Zig Ziglar. Copyright Thomas Nelson Publishers, Nashville, Tennessee.*

Zig Ziglar has written ten celebrated books on personal growth, faith, leadership, family and success. He has shared the speaking platform with such distinguished Americans as Presidents Ford, Reagan and Bush, Generals Norman Schwarzkopf and Colin Powell, Dr. Norman Vincent Peale and numerous congressmen and governors. His Zig Ziglar Corporation, a huge professional training company, is based in Carrollton, Texas, where he also teaches a Sunday school class at his local church.

Chapter 9

The Joy of Helping Others

I tell you the truth, whatever you did for one of the least of these brothers of mine, you did for me. (Matthew 25:40)

Kinder Than Kind

Jerry B. Jenkins

The following is not a "bounce back" story as such. Nor is God or Jesus even mentioned once, although the term "Christian" is used twice. Why, then, is it in this book? Because these touching accounts of Christlike ministry are so suffused with the essence and thrust of Jesus' earthly ministry that a sense of His presence is inescapable in all the author describes. Helping others to "bounce back," i.e., to overcome adversity—physical, spiritual or otherwise—is a high calling. Indeed, it is Jesus' specific call to each one of us. —DLJ

When the Francis Schaeffer film and book *How Shall We Then Live?* hit Chicago in the 1970s, I joined more than 4,000 at the Aerie Crown Theater at McCormick Place to see it.

Dr. Schaeffer was also there in person, and at the end of the film, the great Christian philosopher and thinker took questions from the audience.

At one point a young man in the balcony began a question in a halting, nearly incoherent growl. Clearly he suffered from cerebral palsy. Dr. Schaeffer closed his eyes in concentration as the question went on and on. I understood maybe one-fourth of the words.

When the man finished, Dr. Schaeffer said, "I'm sorry, I didn't understand the last three words."

The young man repeated them. "Forgive me," Dr. Schaeffer said, "the last word again, please."

After the young man repeated it, Dr. Schaeffer restated his question and answered it with the time and dignity he had accorded all the other questions. When the young man asked yet another lengthy question, some in the audience shook their heads, as if irritated that he should take so much time.

But Dr. Schaeffer repeated the process, being sure he understood every word and answering fully. It struck me that he had been kinder than the incident called for. He could have asked someone else to interpret for him. He could have asked to speak to the young man later. But everything he had expounded in his book and film was tested by this seemingly insignificant incident.

He had been kinder than kind.

A few years ago, my wife and I attended a writers' conference. We were in the cafeteria, conversing with a local pastor and his wife, when a lady with cerebral palsy was wheeled to the table and her tray of food set before her.

The pastor greeted her as if her joining us was a highlight of his day. He introduced her all around and joked with her. Somehow it came out that they had met just two days before.

The rest of us sat there trying to avoid embarrassing her, not looking as she awkwardly pushed the food around on her plate, spilled most of it on its way to her mouth and left most of that on her face. Her new friend, the pastor, took it in stride.

He didn't look away. Without fanfare he casually put his own spoon at the edge of her plate so she could scoop her mashed potatoes without losing them. He looked at her when he talked to her, and when too much food accumulated on her face, he casually wiped it away with his own napkin.

He would have been kind simply to have included her, talked to her and treated her as a peer. But he had nurtured her, protected her, helped her without making a show of it. He had been kinder than kind.

A couple of years ago I was at a convention waiting to chat with Roosevelt Grier, the massive former pro football player, now a minister. Just before I got to him, a woman brought her young teen son, who clearly had Down's Syndrome, for a handshake and an autograph from Rosey.

The big man could have simply smiled, shaken hands and signed. But he did more. He dropped to one knee, putting him at eye level with the boy. Rosey put his arm around him, pulled him close and spoke to him quietly. I couldn't help myself. I edged closer.

"Are you a Christian?" Rosey asked.

"Yes, sir."

"Praise the Lord. Can I pray with you?"

The boy was overcome. All he could do was nod. As they prayed, the mother wept. When she tried to thank Rosey, he simply winked at her. Then, to the boy, he said, "You take care of your mama now, you hear?"

"Yes, sir."

Oh, that we might all be caught being kinder than kind.

Excerpted from Life Flies When You're Having Fun, *Jerry B. Jenkins. Originally published in Moody magazine. Used by permission.*

 Jerry B. Jenkins is a former Vice President for Publishing at Moody Bible Institute and Editor of *Moody* magazine. He is the author of more than 100 books (three of which were *New York Times* bestsellers) including the best-selling *Left Behind* novel series. His writing has appeared in *Reader's Digest*, *Parade* and dozens of Christian periodicals. He has written numerous biographies, including books with Hank Aaron, Bill Gaither, Luis Palau, Walter Payton and Nolan Ryan. He considers it "the privilege of a lifetime" to have assisted Billy Graham with his memoirs, *Just As I Am*. He and his wife and three sons live in Zion, Illinois. Contact him at Alive Communications Literary Agency, Suite 329, 1465 Kelly Johnson Blvd., Colorado Springs, CO 80920.

These Are My Children

Beverly Hamel

I just couldn't believe it had happened again. "Please, God, not another miscarriage!" I gasped. I wondered how I could go through a *sixth* miscarriage. But it was all so true.

I couldn't keep control of myself all that day. It became even worse in the days following. The short (three-and-a-half-week) pregnancy had broken down my immune system. I had ear and sinus infections as well as headaches. Many faithful sisters were praying for me almost nonstop.

The illness cleared but another "infection" followed—one of the heart and mind. It attacked me in the form of bitterness and anger. I questioned the Lord's goodness and mercy. My prayers were hollow and ineffective. I even shut out those closest to me—I couldn't bear to receive from them.

In the Bible bookstore where I worked, every time I heard a child call, "Mommy, where are you?" or "Oh, look, Daddy!" or "Can I have it?" it would tear me up. It was hard to go to work in the store and listen to it every day.

Months went by like that, and as Mother's Day loomed, I began to loathe the thought of it: the tributes, the flowers, the children singing as they passed out roses, the men's choir singing love songs to their wives.

When that day arrived I had to talk myself into going to church. It was a good thing I went: That day God began a new work in me.

My pastor, John Vertifuele, called on all the mothers to stand (of course!), but then he called on all the single and childless women to stand as well. (That was different.) He told us that, although we have no children by blood, we have children by the blood of Jesus.

"As these children crawl around your skirts in the lobby, in the back of their minds they recognize you as women of God," he said. By our example, he pointed out, many children look to us and can learn God's ways from us.

A few weeks later, as I was worshiping the Lord at the church door where I usher, I felt the Lord telling me to open my eyes. I did. Watching me from her mother's arms was a little baby girl. *See, Bev? You are helping this mother to train her daughter to worship and love Me,* He said. I knew then that I wasn't really barren. I never was.

He reminded me of my years in Sunday school teaching the Word to Southeast Asian children. Although many people had commented about it, I had never felt that I was those children's mother.

But now, my eyes were opened and great joy flowed in—these *were* my children!

But God was not finished with me; He knew that another new work must begin, and begin He did—two months later. I now knew motherhood, but now I was to know *Fatherhood* in a wholly different light.

I still fought to pray and worship the Lord, but it felt hollow. I held on to the verse that says we walk by faith and not by sight. I knew the Lord heard me, but there didn't seem to be an answer.

One morning, while listening to praise and worship music while dressing for work, I heard the Lord say to me in my heart: *Why don't you speak to Me, Bev?*

"But Jesus, I am talking to You," I said.

He replied, *I am your Father.*

I couldn't understand. But then He showed me He wanted me to relate to Him, not only as Jesus, but as Father God.

I thought of my earthly father. Sweet images of home life—Thursday night homecomings, when Daddy would arrive from "out of town"—popped into my mind. Daddy had nine children and was forced to go miles to support us. The air was festive—Momma singing her silly ditty of "Daddy's Comin' Home"; food cooking; we kids with dancing eyes waiting to hear the car door slam; taking his thermos into the kitchen; hearing his big heavy boots drop to the floor. All was as it should be—Daddy's home.

I was reared in a faith that taught us to pray to

God through Mary. Later I learned to talk directly to Jesus, just as Scripture teaches. But all during my prayer life I had never felt I was talking to God as Father. Now, God reminded me of what Jesus said in John 10:30 and 14:9: "I and the Father are one. . . . Anyone who has seen me has seen the Father." He wanted to be with me as *Father*.

As Father, the Lord began to show me the facets of parenthood. He shared His feelings of a son leaving home, of a son rejected, of the anguish of a dying son. *See, dear,* I felt Him saying, I *also had a Son who died. He is risen forever, and so is your child.*

It is a sobering feeling to know that we can relate to Father God's experiences. Truly, we are made in His own likeness. With such a legacy, we can no longer claim that we are childless, without family or forgotten. "How great is the love the Father has lavished on us, that we should be called children of God!" (1 John 3:1). And so we are!

Beverly Hamel was born and grew up in Kansas City, Missouri. She and her husband, Gary, now reside in San Diego, California. For eleven years, she taught outdoor Bible studies to children from Southeast Asia. Other than an article for the Christian Book Association's *Marketplace*, this is her first published work.

The Turning Point

Leila McDougal

Uneasy thoughts about my husband, Knute, crowded my mind that morning in February 1950. I had just put Katie, our almost-two-year-old daughter, down for her nap. Knute was home, pacing the floor as though looking for a way out of a trap, as in truth he was.

I knew he was hurting. The liquor he had relied on for years as a panacea for ills and problems now had him panicked. His strained look revealed not only his physical pain, but an inner struggle as well.

I glanced out the window. Dark clouds hovered and the wind lashed and swirled the scattered leaves around the trees in the yard.

Knute walked to the kitchen. He poured a cup of coffee. With his elbows leaning on the table, he rested his head in his hands and muttered, "What am I going to do?"

I wished I had a blueprint to offer, one he could accept, but I had learned that suggestions when he was drinking were not well received. So I tried to encourage him, "You'll find a way. You always have."

And he always had, dealing with every obstacle put in his path. In my heart, though, I feared this adversary was more fiendish than any he'd ever faced before.

He took my hand. At last he broke the silence. "I have to go," he said softly. As he rose from the table he put his hand to his side and said through clenched teeth, "My liver really hurts."

Only then did I burst out, "Shouldn't you see Dr. Davis? You could do that."

He put on his coat and his earmuffed cap, then threw his arm around my shoulder. I held him close.

At the sound of the wind howling at the windows, I motioned toward the window and murmured, "It's awfully stormy."

But I let him go. I watched him go down the steps, saw the wind whip at his great enveloping coat as he moved uncertainly down the walk and out to his car. He turned and waved. I waved back.

Then I stretched up my arms, as if to release something, and breathed the words, "God, I am turning him over to You. He is so ill and too drink-ridden to drive. Please, please take care of him."

I wanted to put it from my mind, but that wasn't easy. Should I call someone and talk? I shook my head. I never had laid my problems on friends and family. I had kept my own counsel in the past, and that's what I'd do now.

Katie awoke and I brought her out for lunch. Then a thought struck me: *What could be better? She wouldn't judge—she'd just smile and love me. I can talk to her!*

"Katie," I said, "you have a great daddy. He loves us, but he's having trouble right now."

I told her how Knute had worked at many jobs and was tops at everything. When we were first married, he did well selling insurance. Then the depression changed everything. After a time we rented a farm, even though he had never farmed before. He made a garden, planted wheat and herded our few scrawny cattle. Later, we moved to town and he began operating coin machines. He added nickelodeons and began making more money than we'd ever seen, so we bought a house.

I didn't tell Katie that for years Knute drank without showing it in his manner, business or driving. He could recover from a binge and stay off drinking for long periods of time. Gradually that changed, and his stays in hospitals were all too frequent. Still, with loyal helpers and a book-keeper, his business did well enough.

I gave Katie some crackers and milk and told her how the war and gas rationing wiped out our business, forcing us to sell our music machines. Then Knute bought the billiard hall/beer parlor. "Katie," I said, "I didn't want that.

"I gave in when your daddy said, 'Tiny, I don't have a profession. I have to do what I can to make a living. I know how to make that pool hall go.' So I gave in.

"Well, he proved to be right," I said. I told her how the customers liked watching him deftly flip the hamburgers, how they raved over his chili, how they relished his sharp wit. It became a bustling place.

I pointed to a picture of Knute on the wall and asked, "Who's that, Katie?"

"Dad-dy," she said, then held her hands above her head and said, "B-i-i-g."

I nodded. "He sure is." Knute towered over most people—and that might have been what helped him manage his place the way he wanted.

After a while the children came from school. It was also Knute's time to eat and see the children. But he hadn't come home. The evening passed. Midnight came, but not Knute. I went to bed, but couldn't sleep.

I never thought I would see the time when Knute was not in control of things, and now I resented spending sleepless nights concerned about such an expert driver making it home safely.

As the night wore on, my mind continued its futile meandering. Life had been good until the last few years. I wondered about that alcoholic recovery program Dr. Meyer had told Knute about. I know the doctor was hoping it would help him save Knute's liver. After we went to that one meeting, why didn't he follow up on it?

Morning came. The children went to school. I waited. About 2 in the afternoon, a man came to the door. I knew him only by sight. He was a house painter and was known to be a hard drinker. Through the screen door, he said, "Knute's OK. He's in good hands."

"Oh, thank you," I said, holding back tears. "Won't you come in?"

"Just for a minute." He stepped inside. "Knute spent last night at Tobe's house. Tobe's got the same problem as Knute and me. But Tobe and I have been driving every week to the recovery program meetings in Hays."

He continued, "Tobe brought Knute to the meeting this morning. I was there. Knute wasn't up to calling you. We're sittin' with him till he gets dried out and feels better." He paused a moment, then went on, "Knute wanted you to know he's OK."

With his hand on the doorknob, he turned back to say, "Oh, yes, don't be surprised if you get a different man back. This program is working for a lot of goners. Well, you won't hear any more until Knute comes home."

After he left, I thought, *If this works, I'll believe God started this organization just for Knute and me.* A great sense of gratitude enveloped me—Knute was physically safe, at least for now.

Knute arrived four days later. That day, February 18, 1950, was his first day of sobriety, which lasted with no slips for the remaining twenty-five years of his life. That day also marked a turning point in my life.

In the days to come, I learned more about the

miracle of the program. Knute and a few others began meeting often. A charter chapter was formed in Colby. It grew. Many a hopeless person found new life with this fledgling group through their enthusiasm and tenacity of purpose.

Mental powers, stability, self-control, congeniality and wit—qualities that had in part deserted these people—resurfaced when they began to take their own recovery inventories. The spouses were thrilled with their newly salvaged mates. I learned that many a wife believed, as I did, that a loving God had created the program just for her, in answer to her prayers.

Yes, God does answer our prayers. The answer may come, as it did in my case, through an outside help organization; it may come through a person or persons God sends our way; or it may come through a change in circumstances that we have not foreseen. If we give our burdens to Him in simple trust, God is faithful to work His will in our lives. I know that to be true.

Be strong and courageous. Do not be terrified; do not be discouraged, for the LORD your God will be with you wherever you go. (Joshua 1:9)

Leila McDougal moved from Kansas to San Diego in 1985. She was a teacher, homemaker and wife for forty-five years. She writes poetry and stories for children based on her early life in Kansas. She is currently working on her autobiography.

Unexpected Curves

Patty Stump

For each of us life brings experiences that impact us. Some experiences may be the fulfillment of long-awaited hopes and dreams, unfolding over time, while others may occur abruptly, bringing unexpected curves to our journey.

A summer missions trip to the Philippines brought a bit of each of these to my life. I had always had an interest in missions and was excited about joining a team for a short-term evangelism outreach.

Our team arrived in the Philippines, and after a brief cultural overview we were divided into pairs and sent out to various locations across the island of Luzon. My teammate and I were delighted to be housed with a Filipino pastor and his family in a small community two hours outside of Manila. The pastor's home consisted of four small rooms and housed a total of eleven people: the Filipino pastor and his wife, their son and a nephew, a housekeeper, four visiting teachers and the two of us.

Cinder block walls divided the main rooms and a small corridor off the kitchen led to the "shower," a large barrel filled with water enclosed in a darkened area. A container was used to pour the water for bathing purposes and a small hole in the center of the floor served as the drain. The corridor and shower areas lit only through the use of flashlights.

Each morning the family's prized rooster announced the dawn with boisterous crowing, awakening the neighborhood. After a simple breakfast consisting of coffee and rice we boarded a colorful "jeepney," which shuttled us to our final destination—the small countryside church from which we served.

Each evening after supper we settled into our bedroom, enclosing ourselves in mosquito netting. Our bedroom door exited into the pastor's family bedroom, where he and the three other members of his family would sleep on the floor each night, carefully keeping watch over us to assure that our safety and personal needs were cared for.

The areas where we served had little or no electricity or running water. Most homes were constructed of plywood, often lacking completed walls and fully covered roofs. As we visited in the homes, we were often served the last remnants of food contained in a household. To preserve the honor of the host, we graciously accepted whatever was offered, savoring both the morsels and the generous hospitality.

One morning, the pastor of our home asked what our favorite foods were in the States. We chatted lightly of our favorite dishes—pizza, tacos and chicken. That evening, as we returned from our day's outing, we smelled the aroma of fried chicken seeping out of the opened windows. What a feast they had prepared!

As the morning sun awakened us the next day, my teammate and I were surprised to have missed the crowing of the faithful family rooster. Over breakfast our comments regarding the absence of our wake-up crow were met with awkward gazes from the pastor and his tiny wife.

Without another word, my teammate and I simultaneously realized that our feathered friend had been the main course of our meal the night before. We knew how deeply they had treasured this animal and found ourselves without words as the pastor and his wife excused themselves from breakfast.

One morning on our scenic ride to the neighboring village, I noticed women alongside the road washing clothes. They scrubbed the clothing while squatting awkwardly over their water basins. I noticed damp clothing on bushes and tree limbs, carefully laid out to dry. Suddenly I saw a shirt that looked familiar, then a skirt, then a row of underwear! Those were *my* clothes strewn alongside the road! That evening, a pile of neatly folded clean clothing sat on the edge of my bed.

What great pains they took in tending to our daily needs.

As summer drew to a close I wasn't sure whose lives had been more impacted—those with whom we'd shared the gospel, or ours. As we prepared to return to the United States, the pastor and his family excitedly prepared a family day trip to a beautiful volcanic peak that overlooked the countryside. We enjoyed a simple lunch together, talking of our summer and of future plans. It was a day of sharing our hearts and the beauty of the countryside—perfect, except for the distraction of a few pesky mosquitoes.

Within a couple of days my teammate and I rejoined the rest of our group in Manila for our debriefing. We shared our experiences and unanimously agreed that we had each been changed over the course of the summer. As we said our farewells, I realized I was feeling unusually weary. Two days later my body ached as if my bones were broken. My head throbbed from a soaring temperature and joint tenderness made even minimal movement quite painful. I was told that I had dengue fever, a disease commonly referred to as "breakbone fever." The mosquito borne virus is common in the Philippines, particularly in the mountainous area where we had our final picnic.

It has been ten years, and still the achiness lingers in my joints. I've made adjustments, trading aerobics and jogging for brisk walking and cutting back on my schedule. While I would delight in finding these symptoms completely gone, they remind me to slow my pace and take time to be still.

Someone asked if I would do it all again. Yes, I would; for the broader issue is keeping the journey in perspective, knowing that life brings unexpected curves and unforeseen hurdles. Yet if we opt out of the experiences, we miss out on the fullness of life.

The Lord reminds us: He takes the changed plans and collided pieces and knits them together for His good and divine purposes.

And we know that in all things God works for the good of those who love him, who have been called according to his purpose. (Romans 8:28)

Patty Stump, M.Ed., C.P.C., is a pastor's wife, mother of two, Christian Marriage and Family Counselor, writer and speaker for women's events, marriage seminars and weekend retreats. She communicates scriptural truths for practical application with humor and wisdom. Contact: c/o Community Church of Joy, 21000 N. 75th Ave., Glendale, Arizona 85308. Phone: (602) 561-0500.

Why Am I Lonely?

Greg Laurie

Do you know what it is like to be lonely—to be hurting, to be rejected? Maybe you were not the big man on campus when you were in school. Perhaps when you were growing up, your parents moved around—so you changed schools as I did and were moving to new neighborhoods so frequently that you never had a chance to form lasting friendships. That's what my upbringing was like. It seemed that more people knew me as "the new kid" than by my first name.

Maybe when they were picking teams for baseball or some other sport, you were always the last one picked. Did you fit into that category? I sure did. Everyone knows what it is like to be lonely—to be ridiculed and cast off.

But here's the good news: When you come into a relationship with Jesus Christ and invite Him into your life, you will never be alone again. *Never.*

He doesn't promise that you will never have another problem. But He promises, under all circumstances, because God has said, "I will never leave you nor forsake you" (Hebrews 13:5, NKJV), that Jesus is there. No matter what you are going through, when you have Jesus Christ in your life, you have Someone who cares. Of course, that will also include the greatest hope of all—that when we die, we will spend eternity with Jesus Christ in heaven.

That was the great hope that a lonely man named Zacchaeus discovered the day he met Jesus.

Zacchaeus was a tax collector. Not only that, but he was the *chief* tax collector. This meant that he most likely was a very lonely and isolated man. The Roman government forced the Jewish people to pay exorbitant taxes to the foreign occupying power of Rome. The Romans hired many to collect taxes—and some of them were Jews. Thus, because of his occupation, Zacchaeus was hated and reviled by his own people because he was a Jew serving the Roman cause.

Interestingly, Jesus did not say, "This guy is a thief." He didn't say, "He is a rip-off artist." Jesus said this lonely man was simply "lost." He wasn't referring to his unpopularity with the people. Jesus was concerned about the state of Zacchaeus' soul.

Because of his lonely and rejected state, Zacchaeus may have thought: *No, Jesus would never call me. God could never change my life. Everyone hates me. God probably hates me too.*

Have you ever felt that way? Have you ever thought that God just didn't love you? Have you ever thought, *He may love good people or lovable people, but not me?*

When I first heard about Jesus Christ, I was so cynical. When someone suggested, "Just ask Jesus into your life and He will forgive you," I thought, *Oh, yeah, sure. I'm probably the one guy God would skip!* I was so afraid of rejection that I believed even God would reject me. But I was wrong.

It is likely that Zacchaeus also did not understand God's unconditional love. He climbed up the tree just before Jesus came along and gazed down at Jesus from the branches of a tree. In his world of treachery and greed, Jesus must have appeared to be different indeed. Something obviously emanated from Him that the tax collector had never seen before—*a look of unconditional love.* Suddenly Jesus stopped, looked up and called out his name: "Zacchaeus, come down! Hurry up! I am coming over to your house for a meal."

What's so important about that moment? It represents the people in our lives whom we think would never be interested in Jesus Christ. If we see someone sitting on the street, down and out, we think, "That person needs to hear the gospel." But if we see another person tooling by in a Rolls Royce, talking on a cellular phone, we might think, "That person would never listen to the gospel." How would we ever break the ice with someone like that? Maybe we could ask to borrow some Grey Poupon. To approach a rich person is much harder—or so it seems.

It's amazing how many affluent people complain of being empty inside. Secretly, they confide they are not really sure whom they can trust to love them for who they are rather than for how much they're worth. Most of us struggle with loneliness from time to time. Here was Zacchaeus—an empty, lonely, guilty man. Jesus reached out to him just as He reaches out to each one of us today.

Some people think they have to clean up their lives first—or at least make a few changes before they can come to Christ. No, we are instructed to come as we are—with all of our sins. Do you think God doesn't know about them? He knows everything we have done. He knows each of us better than we know ourselves. And He still loves us.

I will not promise you that if you receive Jesus Christ into your life, you will never face difficulties. What I *will* promise you—on the authority of the Bible—is that if you receive Him into your life, you will never be lonely again. Jesus has promised to His own children, "Lo, I am with you always, even to the end of the age" (Matthew 28:20, NKJV). You have His Word on it. You can take that to the bank!

Greg Laurie is Senior Pastor of Harvest Christian Fellowship in Riverside, California—one of the ten largest churches in America. He has authored several books including: *The New Believers Growth Book*, *Giving God Your Best* and *The Great Compromise*. Millions of people have heard him speak at his "Harvest Crusades" conducted all across the country.

About the compiler

Diana L. James' articles and stories have appeared in several national magazines, numerous local and regional publications and in seven anthology books. She is editor/compiler of her own book, *Bounce Back* (Horizon Books, 1997), to which this book is a companion. Diana hosted a TV interview program for five years. She was a member of National Speakers Association for five years. She has been on the staff of CLASS (Christian Leaders, Authors and Speakers Seminars) for nine years and speaks for churches, retreats, women's conferences and bereavement groups. E-mail her at DianaJames@aol.com